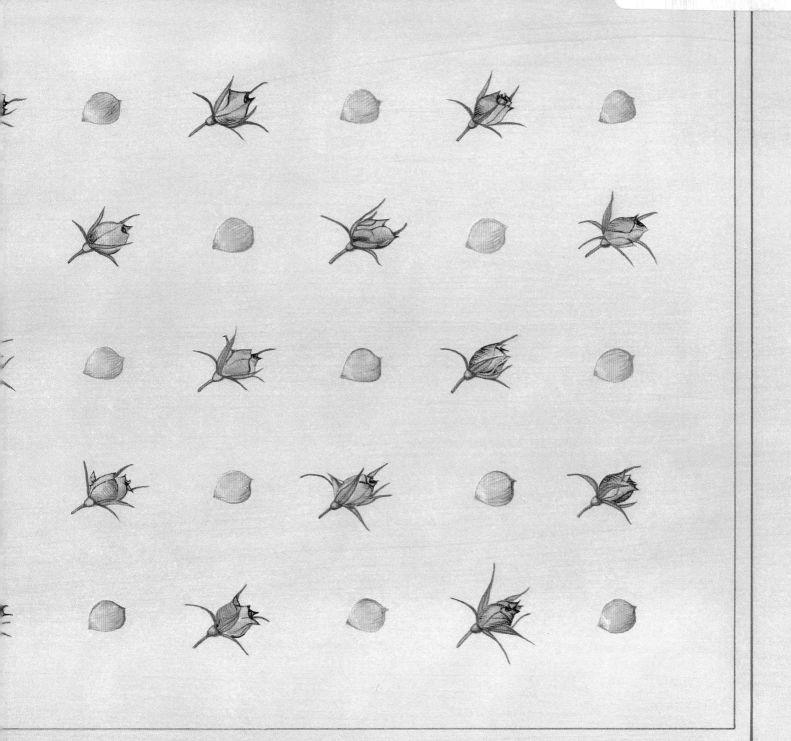

THE GARDEN AT ASHTREE COTTAGE

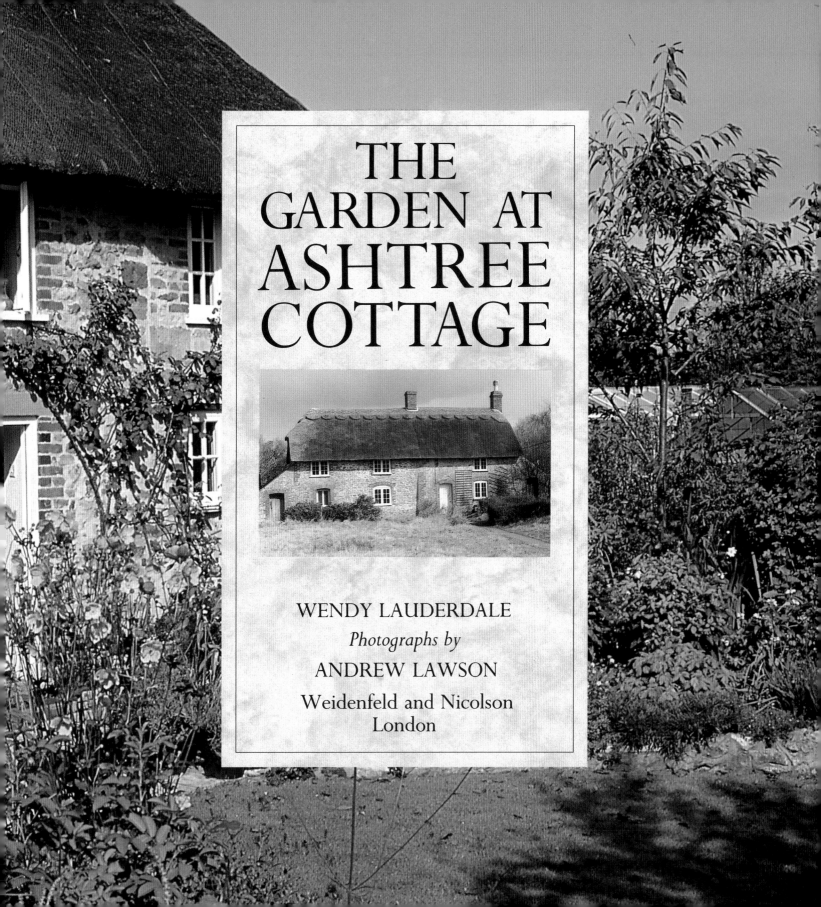

THE GARDEN AT ASHTREE COTTAGE

WENDY LAUDERDALE

Photographs by

ANDREW LAWSON

Weidenfeld and Nicolson
London

To my dear friend Gwen Beaumont, who has been my inspiration and mentor for many years, and to the memory of my mother, who first sowed the seed.

Text and photographs on pp 9, 10, 22 and 44 © Wendy Lauderdale 1993

All other photographs © Andrew Lawson 1993

First published in 1993 by George Weidenfeld and Nicolson Ltd,
Orion House, 5 Upper St Martin's Lane, London WC2H 9EA

British Library Cataloguing-in-Publication Data
A catalogue record for this book is available from the British Library

Design by Isobel Gillan
Illustrations by Joanne Cowne

ISBN 0–297–83209–3

Typeset by Deltatype Ltd, Ellesmere Port
Printed and bound in Italy

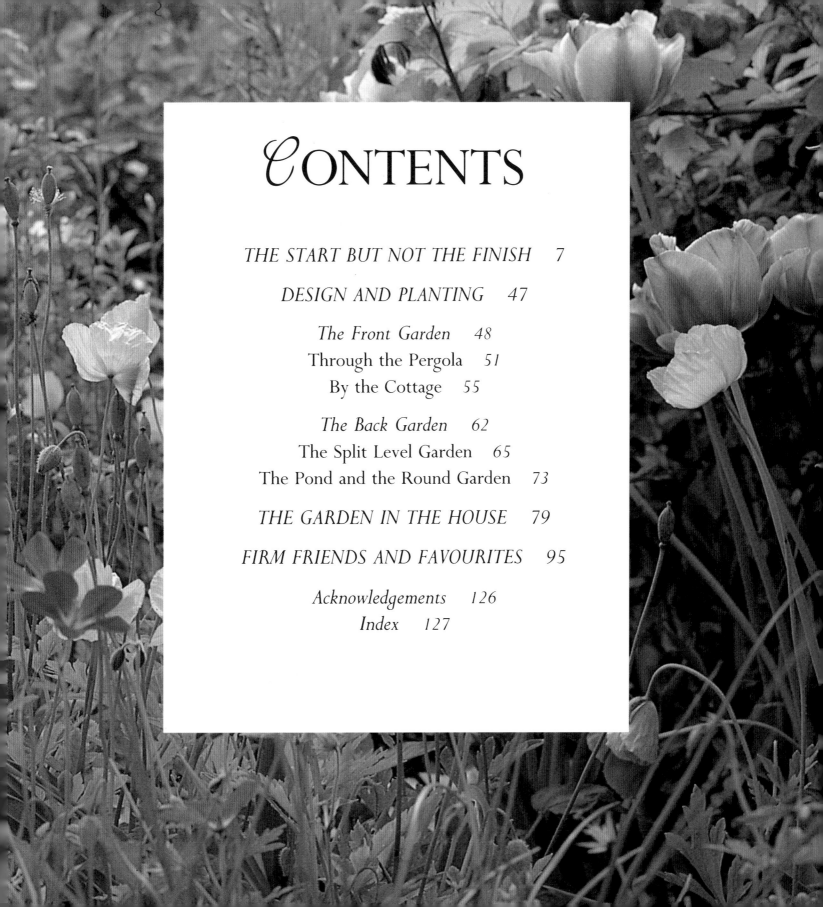

CONTENTS

THE START
— BUT NOT —
THE FINISH

M Y FIRST SIGHT of Ashtree Cottage and its 'garden' was on a bleak winter's day in January some eight years ago. We were having to move house because my husband Len had recently been made redundant, so we decided to drive out to have a look at this National Trust-owned property near Stourhead House and Gardens in Wiltshire, some twenty miles (32 km) from our Somerset home. I remember well my first reaction. Both cottage and garden looked so forlorn, neglected and unloved, but viewing this poor derelict garden, even in the depths of winter, I felt drawn to it by its potential and promise.

After that first view we returned on a number of occasions, fighting our way through the under-growth outside and negotiating rather dubious floorboards in the house. More and more the prospect of making a garden here began to appeal to me. For the first time I should have some space in which to grow many of those delectable plants I had seen in nurseries, growing in other people's gardens and featured in books and catalogues. Although often tempted, I rarely bought or looked at garden-ing books in those days, as I had only a pocket-handkerchief-sized garden and was a very frustrated gardener, with insufficient space in which to grow all the lovely plants these books featured. More often than not when I did succumb and buy a coveted

plant I would end up having to give it away to friends. I think too that I felt somewhat intimidated, sure I could never achieve anything like the wonderful gardens and planting schemes depicted in books. Everything always looked so perfect. I now realize that no photographer is going to submit a photograph of anything that doesn't look at its best. I remember once taking heart from reading that one renowned gardener – I think it was Vita Sackville-West – said that you cannot expect every part of your garden to be looking at its best all the time but that the important thing was always to have some part of it at its peak and providing interest.

Our offer for the lease on the property was accepted by the National Trust in March. We asked their permission to start work on the garden while the legalities of the purchase were churning through the system, and to our delight they agreed with alacrity. We put our house on the market and by the beginning of April had set about clearing the wilderness at Ashtree Cottage. I don't think we had any idea of the size of the task we were undertaking, as we set about it with our bare hands and with little equipment bar the basic range of garden tools. I didn't really have any preconceived notions, either, as to the ultimate shape and design of the garden. It was simply a question of starting at one point, working our way round and putting ideas into play

A priority was to create a nursery area in which to accommodate my first acquisitions for eventual planting in the garden.

as they suggested themselves. However, my first thoughts were to prepare a small area which could serve as a nursery bed for plants I could bring from our previous garden, bits and pieces given me by friends, and any plants I might buy from nurseries and garden centres.

The ground in front of the cottage – an area about 30 yards (27 m) wide and stretching about 50 yards (45 m) from the entrance – was really no more than a field of tussock grass with a healthy crop of dandelions and thistles and very little else. In it stood a wonderful gnarled, lichen-covered umbrella-shaped apple tree, one or two very tired and elderly roses, and the hallmarks of almost every old cottage garden – forsythia, tangled honeysuckle, flowering currant (*Ribes*), and a clump of red paeonies almost buried under the grass. A narrow tarmac path, sited off-centre, cut through the field to the front door of the cottage where its little porch was hanging on

drunkenly to one side – more in hope than in conviction of its salvation. In fact not much more than a nudge dislodged it for all time into a crumpled heap! To one side of the cottage was a derelict, overgrown area with old blackcurrant and gooseberry bushes, and a miniature forest of brambles so dense that the blackbirds had taken up residence and were busy rearing their young. It became obvious that this area would have to wait a while, at least until the young birds had flown.

The back garden appeared to have been the main rubbish tip of the property and once again was totally overgrown with brambles, nettles, old raspberry canes, and elderberry and wild plum trees in abundance. There was an inordinate amount of rubbish which was not immediately apparent, as much of it had been there for so long that it was covered up with a generous blanket of moss and nettles. One of our main concerns was as to the

Clearing the overgrown back garden of all its rubbish and brambles was a daunting and challenging task.

whereabouts of inevitable wells, and whether they had been filled in, or whether one of us might suddenly disappear from view. What was obvious was that there had never been any cultivation of this area as a flower garden. I believe the previous occupants, a wheelwright and his large family, may well have kept livestock, and there had certainly been some kind of a workshop, as we found a very dilapidated shed with the last remnants of the wheelwright's trade. Our first job was to clear the worst of the undergrowth, which meant a lot of bonfires. Quite naturally this didn't endear us to some of the neighbours as there was so much rubbish to be disposed of, and the wind – for which Kilmington, at its altitude of around 780 feet (135 m), is renowned – was not always kind to us or, should I say, to the neighbours.

There were only a couple of things that I knew with any certainty that I really wanted in the garden: a pond of some description was an essential; and I also felt that we should have a pergola going at least part of the way down the path leading from the entrance to the cottage. I had a vision of a tunnel effect in a haze of blues which would be perfumed at every step, and as I love delphiniums I visualized them here. It was another year before we were able to embark on this project, but there was plenty to keep us occupied in the meantime. I'm not one of those people with a far-reaching vision of a garden, who can sit down at the outset and draw a plan of what it will ultimately look like. I have to live with it and let it evolve slowly. Each move I make, be it drawing out the vague outline of a border or planting a tree or shrub, seems to suggest the next step. I like to be able to start with a clean canvas, and work from a very general outline of what I want, both in terms of the plants I'd like to grow and the uses to which I might want to put the garden. I never considered that one day I would be opening this particular garden to the public or, indeed, that it would give so much pleasure to so many people other than myself.

Few of us have much experience when we first set out to make a garden and our knowledge is often limited, so it is only with time and practice that we learn what we want. This practice often involves failure as well as success, disappointment as well as joy, but nature is very generous and tolerant; and with patience, hard work and dedication, and an element of luck, we can all achieve good results in our gardens. The larger the variety of plants we try to grow, the wider our knowledge becomes, and we get a better idea of not only which plants will flourish in the conditions in our own garden, but which ones we actually want to include.

As yet no-one in my family has shown much indication of being a gardener, but we all enjoy and use the garden. Weather permitting, in the summer months we virtually live outside from breakfast to supper and often late into the night, with perhaps a few candles flickering, as we enjoy the wonderful perfumes that float on the night air, particularly after a hot summer's day or after a fresh shower of rain. We are also most fortunate here in having the house set well back from the road, with fields behind us. Like any amateur I've made a lot of errors, largely out of total ignorance at the outset, but I believe this is how we learn. In fact, the more I learn, the more I realize how little I know, and the more dissatisfied I become with my efforts, since I am increasingly aware of my mistakes. I'm not tempted to give up, however, because the satisfaction and the joy I derive from my garden outweigh any other emotion. But I do ask myself sometimes why we are a nation of gardeners, when we have to struggle against the elements to keep our treasures alive through bad winters, perhaps only to have them shrivel up in an unexpected drought in the summer. It's certainly a challenge and there is also so much variety – maybe that is why we keep at it. Len and I have spent most of our married life overseas in tropical countries, where bougainvilleas, hibiscus, tecomas, and zinnias provide wonderful splashes of exotic colours, but where gardening lacked the excitement and expectation that I experience here.

When we started work on the garden at Ashtree Cottage, I made most of the borders that are now in place, but they have changed radically over the years in shape, size and planting schemes. They were far too narrow initially, and I definitely overplanted them. Even now I'm forever moving things, because I have decided either they are in the wrong place or they have fulfilled the job they were planted to do. I often refer to my garden as being 'nomadic', as it is permanently on the move. I don't think you should ever be frightened to move things, or dig them out altogether, for there's no point in keeping a plant in a particular position if it isn't right there or you have grown tired of it and want something different. I am continually widening the borders, largely to accommodate the ever-increasing number of plants I keep acquiring, but also because our soil is predominantly greensand, which, as its name suggests, is a very light, sandy soil, and very stony. It encourages a lot of moss, and the edges of the borders collapse easily with this combination of moss and stones, so to keep them sharp and neat I am always having to cut them away. Having wider borders and a little less lawn doesn't necessarily make the garden look smaller; it is a matter of getting the proportions and balance right.

We were blessed with wonderful weather in the spring and summer of the year we started working on the garden, which enabled us to work uninterrupted several days a week, bringing picnics with us to enjoy under the old apple tree and often staying on late into the night to make full use of the long summer evenings. In that time we managed to clear nearly all the areas of the garden and mapped out most of the main features. There were certain areas which I wasn't sure about, so these were left until I had a better idea of how I wanted them to develop.

We planted a number of fruit trees in the larger of the two lawns in the front garden, making in effect a small orchard, more for the blossom in the spring than the harvest in the autumn, and then we planted up the borders with a mixture of trees, shrubs and herbaceous plants. We decided that the area to the side of the house, where I had made my initial nursery bed, would be the kitchen garden.

To the rear of the cottage the lie of the land suggested we could have a split level. There were far too many wild plum and elderberry trees, and an enormous privet tree, so many of these could come out. It was obvious that an ordinary rotivator would not be enough for the job of levelling the ground, and we obtained the help of two local farm workers, who brought in a tractor to haul out tree stumps and roots and generally turn over and level the area. They then proceeded to prepare it for seeding down to lawn later on in the autumn. In this area one of them also constructed a small curved dry-stone wall about 12 inches (30 cm) high, which created two

ABOVE *The glowing fruit of the dessert apple 'Spartan' taste as good as they look.*

RIGHT *A white-flowering Japanese cherry,* Narcissus *'Thalia' and* Tulipa *'Purissima' create a white garden immediately in front of the cottage in spring.*

levels. To one side under the trees a hole was scooped out by the tractor to form what would eventually be the pond. At the time this hole looked quite substantial and more than adequate to make a nice water feature – one of my misjudgements. Now that the garden has grown up and developed all round it, it looks almost ridiculously small – in summer it is scarcely visible – and I affectionately call it my 'puddle'. However the frogs love it, and it has been a very productive maternity ward for them during the last few springs. We have a permanent encampment of them in and around it, feasting off the slugs and snails in the vicinity. The hostas I grow here keep in very good shape, unlike others in the garden which so often end the summer in tatters from snail damage. The blackbirds use the pond margins for bathing in the early morning, often queuing up for best vantage points, and the dragonflies swoop and dive over it in the summer. The pond nestles under the plum trees but I subsequently learnt that, strictly speaking, ponds should not be sited under trees. I find it natural and evocative of my childhood: as children in Sussex we were often taken for walks in the beech woods where there were ponds overhung with trees and where we used to fish with a bent pin on the end of a piece of string – history doesn't recall whether or not we ever caught anything, though somehow I doubt it. But siting a pond under trees does have its disadvantages, in that the trees take all the moisture from the surrounding ground, so it's a bit of a struggle to keep the kinds of plants that thrive in damp situations looking healthy and happy. Every now and then in the summer I flood the pond to give everything around it a good drink. One day I plan to enlarge it and have a generous water margin in which to grow bogside plants like primulas, filipendulas, astilbes and iris, which revel in that situation.

We didn't do much more to the front garden in that first year, but elsewhere shapes and lines slowly began to evolve and paths were made around the house and through the garden and vegetable area. More and more plants were acquired and were found a home. That was only the beginning but I remember saying to Len at the end of that first summer: 'Now I've got all the plants I want'. I dread to think how many thousands of plants ago that was! Among those that I had brought with me were a number that proved very generous in their perform-ance and their production of offspring, revelling in the wonderful virgin soil they were being treated to. Varieties of *Phlox paniculata*, delphiniums, violas, polemoniums (Jacob's ladder), sweet Williams, cam-panulas and many others were planted in repetitive groups in the borders. After a couple of years, when I was finding nurseries more and more irresistible – I simply couldn't keep away – I soon discovered I needed more space, so not only did the borders get wider, but I started to thin out and discard quite a number of these repetitive groups. I gave away as much as I could find a home for – I've always hated having to throw plants away – and our vegetable garden began to be taken over by rows of delphi-niums for picking, and other 'bits and pieces' which I found myself potting up. The garden is now open under the National Gardens Scheme and also by appointment on other days, and it seems there is nothing people like more when they visit a garden than to be able to go home with something they have actually seen growing there. We no longer have lovely fresh home-grown vegetables but rows of pots of different shapes and sizes, and I have even more of an excuse to go prowling around the nurseries looking for new treasures. Nurseries are to me what

The pond in early summer before the surrounding plants have all but obscured it from view.

sweet shops must be to a chocoholic. Somebody once commented that gardening and buying plants are a disease for which there is no known cure!

There was a lot of talk and enthusiasm at that time for the white border so I decided that perhaps I ought to have one too, and set about trying to replan and replant the long, north-facing border in the front garden. Somehow it didn't seem to come off, and I asked myself why I was trying to mimic other people's ideas – much better to 'do my own thing'. I decided that although it is good to get ideas and inspiration from the experience and expertise of others who have succeeded, your own garden is such a personal thing that you should put the stamp of your own personality into it. After all it is your garden, so you should make it first and foremost to please yourself and not feel you have to follow current fashion. I am very much an instinctive person, be it in gardening, cooking or anything else I attempt to do, and I often find that if I go against my natural instincts, things tend to go awry. I feel too that you really need a large garden to follow rigid colour schemes. Nature seems to produce a predominance and abundance of certain hues in different seasons and a small garden cannot really afford the luxury of waiting for one glorious and sometimes brief showing in any one major area – though, admittedly, there are white and silver shrubs and flowers that will provide cover for a long period.

To return to my brief attempt to create a white border in the front garden, I had already planted there a number of shrubs and herbaceous perennials which just happened to be silver or white. *Elaeagnus angustifolia* 'Caspica'; *Cynara cardunculus* – the wonderful architectural ornamental artichoke;

Stachys lanata (lamb's ears); white phlox and polemoniums; and the beautiful cool, almost ghostly, late-summer-flowering *Lysimachia ephemerum*; but there were also delphiniums, purple sage, and phlox of predominantly mauve and blue shades. As time has gone on, this theme has more or less continued, but what I didn't consider initially was that this border faces due north, is damp and gets rather less sun than elsewhere in the garden, so was not really suitable for silver-leaved plants, some of which decided they really weren't happy and disintegrated. Most silver plants revel in hot, dry, sunny, sometimes even starved conditions. Happily most things have survived, and in some cases actually thrived, and I've been able to add more shade- and moisture-loving plants over the years, like cimicifugas (bugbane), Japanese anemones and hydrangeas for late-summer and autumn flowering, which also perform well with their foliage through the earlier months.

Following that first glorious spring, summer and autumn we had the most ferocious winter and got our first taste of the Kilmington climate. It's almost as if we have our own micro-climate here. The snow lingers long after it has thawed just a mile down the road, the winds come sweeping off the downs, and we always seem to be degrees colder than anywhere else. This has the effect of delaying growth in the garden for anything up to three weeks later than surrounding areas but strangely the autumn seems to be prolonged as well before the onset of winter. Being high the frost disperses fairly rapidly, but the biting winds cause so much damage in winter and spring. In fact our first three winters here were devastating in the garden, and I began to wonder if I should ever be able to grow evergreens, for they kept

Cynara cardunculus, Elaeagnus angustifolia 'Caspica', phlox, delphiniums, white campanulas and polemoniums share the north-facing border in the front garden.

being killed before I could get them established. In the cottage, too, we suffered with the wind getting in under the thatch and freezing the plumbing, causing burst pipes and their attendant problems. I have learnt my lesson now, and no matter how tempted I am, I don't plant anything that is remotely tender or plants that, as the books and catalogues describe them, 'require a warm wall' – we don't have any warm walls, in fact we don't have any warm corners at all.

When we decided to have the pergola constructed – over a year after our initial assault on the garden – I searched through a number of books for illustrations to get some ideas about the design, but didn't have much success. Recently pergolas have become very popular – they seem to be cropping up like mushrooms in gardens everywhere – and there is more choice of design and materials. I had a rough idea in my mind but wasn't exactly sure what I wanted, so it was difficult to convey precise instructions to the man building it for us. When it was finished, my initial reaction was: 'Help! What have I done?' It was immediately christened 'the bridge over the River Kwai'. However, with a few modifications and the planting up of the beds running along either side of it, I realized that its stark outline would soon soften up. Already I could picture it clothed in roses, clematis and honeysuckle. We didn't bring it right to the front door, for this had been moved from its original position when the house was renovated, and was no longer at the foot of the existing path. Instead the pergola ended about three-quarters of the way down the garden. It was another year before I decided that where it ended, it should join up at right-angles on either side with a

Looking down the pergola festooned with roses and underplanted with Viola cornuta*, nepeta and* Anthemis cupaniana*. Tall spires of delphiniums stand sentinel.*

Len performs the never-ending task of deadheading roses and removing blackspot-infected leaves.

3-foot (1 m)-high post and rail fence made of the same tanalized timber as the pergola. This fence would enclose a separate garden immediately in front of the cottage. Early on we had decided not to replace the turf in the front garden but to try and improve what was there, by keeping it cut regularly, filling in as many of the furrows as possible with surplus earth and turf dug from the newly made borders, and subsequently weedkilling and feeding it at least a couple of times a year. Now they pass for quite reasonable lawns, perhaps not your average billiard table, but acceptable nonetheless in their particular location. However, we decided that the areas enclosed by the fence merited a bit more

attention, so we had them weedkilled, rotivated, levelled and sown with grass seed. We then re-sited the existing path from the end of the pergola, in a gentle curve, to the new front door as I felt that a path leading to a thatched cottage should somehow curve or wind at some stage of its journey.

Len takes care of the lawns, and does a wonderful job. So often the lawn cutters and rose sprayers, and odd-job men are the unsung heroes of gardens. These time-consuming jobs are ones I personally find very tedious, so I'm delighted to be able to delegate them and many other chores into Len's hands. He is not a gardener but the help and support he has given me in the making and maintenance of this garden have been invaluable. Having two keen gardeners in a family is not always a good thing, unless their ideas coincide completely, and may result in one of them giving up or, like having two cooks in a kitchen, the production of a real 'dog's dinner'! Returning to the lawns for a moment, I believe their quality, or lack of it, is of paramount importance. If they're in good condition you may not always notice them, but they serve to show off to best advantage the planted areas and furthermore stand up to the wear and tear of people and animals, and whatever the weather throws at them. This has really been born out on the days when we have had our garden open for charity and have had over two hundred people wandering around. By evening there has scarcely been any evidence of this apart from the grass perhaps looking a little flattened. Lawns are the carpets of the garden, and no matter how beautiful the 'furniture' it cannot be shown off to its best advantage if the carpets are stained and worn and threadbare. That's not to say they have to be like putting greens, but free of moss and weed wherever possible.

When we were creating the borders in the early days I wasn't familiar with the magical powers of systemic weedkillers which destroy offending weeds without harming the soil. We dug them all by hand and picked out and burnt every bit of bindweed, couch grass, thistles and nettles that we came across. It was a backbreaking but worthwhile job and it paid off, but it may have something to do with why Len blanches visibly if I ever ask him to do any digging for me now. Happily the days of serious digging are over, but I still wish I had more space waiting to be transformed and cultivated.

Throughout that first summer and autumn the new beds were weeded, sometimes as much as three times a week. It was rather like painting the Forth Bridge: as soon as the end was reached, it was time to start at the beginning again – the weeds enjoying the lovely quality soil as much as the cultivated plants did. It has been quite an uphill struggle against weeds as most of the garden is surrounded by banks, which on our arrival were truly wild and overrun with nettles and bindweed. These banks I continue to spot-weedkill as much as possible as they are quite steep and constant handweeding causes them to collapse more and more. Along with the resident ivy, which I just keep under control, I have now planted them with ground-cover plants to help hold them together, useful plants like *Ajuga reptans* 'Atropurpurea' (bugle); *Alchemilla mollis* (lady's mantle); *Rubus calycinoides*; and *Tolmiea menziesii* 'Taff's Gold' (piggyback plant), often grown as a house plant but perfectly hardy in the garden. The boundary at the back of the garden gives on to a field and the seeds of many of the weeds there continue to invade ininvited. A useful tip I have learned concerning banks is that if you site borders in front of them it is always worthwhile allowing a generous space, say about 3 feet (1 m), at the back to allow easy access to weed, cut hedges, prune shrubs or stake tall perennials there, rather than having to fight your way through the plants from the front which can cause damage.

The celandines are omnipresent in Kilmington as in many other rural areas, and although they are very pretty as a wild flower and light up many a country hedgerow and roadside early in the spring, they can be a nuisance in a garden, particularly once they invade the beds and lawns which they do only too readily, stifling everything in their wake. I've heard it said that a weed is merely a plant in the wrong place but I wonder what distinguishes a weed from a wild flower. Nobody would complain, I imagine, about a proliferation of primroses and cowslips in their garden, though dandelions are never as welcome, and yet cowslips are as prolific here as any dandelion

would be if it were allowed. What is lovelier in late spring than the sight and smell of a bank clothed in cowslips? I originally bought a few little plants and now have a carpet of them on a gently sloping bank. Sadly, dry summers have somewhat decimated the primroses that were always such a welcome early visitor on the banks.

One of the features in the garden when we came was a beech tree, planted rather too dangerously close to the house, but beautiful all the year round nonetheless. In summer it provides dense, cool shade, which cries out for shade-loving plants. Unfortunately so many of these require moisture,

which is rarely available in the shade created by trees. I haven't come across many interesting dry-shade-tolerant plants, so I have decided to risk it and have planted some that require a bit more moisture than the site can realistically provide. During a dry period in the summer I make an effort to see that it gets a little extra watering from time to time. In many ways plants are like children and usually respond to that little extra bit of love and care. If not, then you have to think again and try another tactic. Some mistakes are not always easily rectified and occasionally more drastic action is needed. We have already had to remove a few trees

LEFT *The beech tree overhanging part of the front garden takes on brilliant autumn colour, while nearby white hydrangeas and* Saxifraga fortunei *light up the shady areas.*

BELOW *Cowslips proliferate on this bank in spring, with primroses, oxslips, polyanthus and wild narcissi.*

and shrubs, usually because they were ill-suited to the position in which we had planted them.

I have a passion for the old shrub roses, and spent hours poring over catalogues and browsing round nurseries looking for them. I planted far more than the garden could realistically accommodate. Many were described as being suitable for a small garden, but nobody told the roses that and they grew with increasing vigour. Some have had to be removed and sent off to good homes with friends. One of my sons, who has wonderfully skilled hands and an artist's eye, is trained as a welder and has made for me most attractive and practical iron supports to put around the shrub roses which enable them to be shown off at their best when heavy with bloom in summer. Many of them have stems that cannot cope with the generosity of their flowers, and often end up falling forward in an ungainly heap with their faces trailing in the mud, particularly in wet weather. The supports provide an attractive architectural feature when the roses are dormant and are all but hidden in the summer months. The joy too is that each rose or shrub can have its own support custom made to suit its own individual requirement of height and spread.

We already had 'the bridge over the river Kwai' and now we were about to add another oriental feature. There was an area in the bottom right-hand corner of the garden which hadn't as yet been tackled and had housed a run for my daughter's rabbit and guinea pig, until we had more accommodating quarters built for them. We decided to build a small sitting area, which we rather grandly call our patio, where we could barbecue and sit out on

ABOVE (LEFT) *The exquisite crumpled-tissue-paper blooms of the shrub rose 'Empress Josephine' with* Lychnis coronaria oculata *in the foreground. Sadly 'Josephine' has no perfume.*

RIGHT *Shrub roses bloom happily in the island bed with scabious and campanulas in high summer.*

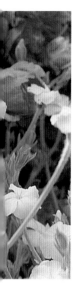

summer evenings. There is a lovely old walnut tree overhanging the area, one of two planted by the previous occupants. This part of the garden had for some years, I think, served as the main rubbish tip, most of which was now buried under the existing bank, and at one stage there had been some kind of dwelling to house a pig or other livestock. It was obvious that a retaining wall would have to be built, but again I failed rather dismally when I tried to convey the size and shape I had in mind to the man who was to build it for us, so it didn't quite emerge as I had envisaged. However with a few subtle changes in shape and with a curve added, we rescued it, but not before it too had acquired a nickname – 'the great wall of China'.

I planted up the raised area behind the wall with some small ground-cover and shrub roses; and where the hedge ended at the walnut tree at one end, leaving an open space on to the field, we covered the ugly barbed wire, put up by the farmer to keep the cows in the field, with split tanalized poles to give a post-and-rail effect. What I didn't appreciate at the time was that this gap would provide an ideal wind tunnel for the bitterly cold easterlies which come sweeping in off Whitesheet Hill – part of the downs north-east of here – or that the moles would, in time, decide that this area would make perfect tunnelling territory. They had a six-acre field in which to tunnel to their hearts' delight, so why should they have to invade my garden?

The roses were not happy in this situation, but the question was where could I move them to. I was rapidly running out of planting space – there were no obvious places for them in the existing borders – so I decided to create a home for them by making a

ABOVE (RIGHT) *The Bourbon rose 'Madame Isaac Pereire'*
bears enormous, richly scented, vivid rose-crimson blooms.

new island bed. This I sited in the lawn in the back garden, to cries from the family of 'Oh no, not another flower bed!' I think the fear was that the garden would eventually consist of flower beds with one or two grass paths running through them, with nowhere to sit or relax. We had already planted a couple of trees in the lawn, so the new bed was designed to accommodate them, one at each end, and laid out in a kidney shape to give the feeling of the lawn running through the planted areas like a winding river. The roses have now settled down happily in the company of tulips in the spring; lilies, scabious and other perennials in the summer; and Japanese anemones, cimicifugas and the lovely tall *Verbena bonariensis* in the autumn.

The mole settlement in the bank behind the wall – although settlement is hardly the appropriate word, as they are anything but settled, always looking for, and finding, new areas in which to wreak their havoc – has been a less-easy problem to solve. The earth keeps sinking and whenever I want to plant anything I come across great gaping holes. It's like pouring water down the plughole if I ever need to water anything. Moles dislike vibration and during the winter and early spring, when there is little or no activity in the garden, particularly before we start mowing the lawns, they become emboldened and are very active. They have tunnelled under the patio and into the surrounding beds and are showing signs of working their way right through into the front garden. So far they haven't ventured into the lawns and this may be due, in part, to the fact that every now and again I go around with the spade, bashing the grass on the edges to create vibrations underground and to act as due warning to them that there is just so much any gardener will tolerate. I've tried a number of remedies including planting euphorbias, pushing garlic cloves down the holes, and purchasing large plastic sunflowers on sticks which are stuck

in the holes and thereby into the tunnels. When the wind rotates the flower it causes vibrations underground. This seems the most effective method but does cause some funny looks from visitors – they could be forgiven for thinking that here was a somewhat eccentric gardener who goes about bashing her lawn with a spade and grows plastic sunflowers! You can also use children's toys – windmills on sticks – placing one in a molehill furthest from your boundary and moving it closer at intervals every few days until hopefully the moles get the message and depart whence they came, or even into the neighbour's garden! The euphorbia method also seems quite effective – its sap is caustic and I imagine the moles instinctively keep well away – although you don't always want large clumps of euphorbias dotted around at random, least of all in your lawn. Moles are such enchanting little creatures

LEFT *An upstairs view of the rear garden, with the small patio that overlooks the fields in the background. Here we enjoy barbecues on summer evenings.*

BELOW *The 'new' island bed was created to provide a home for some small shrub roses which needed to be moved. Narcissi and tulips provide spring interest before the roses bloom.*

but can cause terrible devastation in a garden – a bit like the weeds, they are charming in the right place.

As a result of the combination of the wind and the moles I have given up any ideas of sophisticated planting behind the patio wall and nature has almost taken over, but very effectively, with only a little bit of help from me. Initially I had planted a *Vinca atropurpurea* together with a couple of violets which had arrived uninvited. These have now taken over. Blue *Anemone blanda*, wild wood anemones, primroses, hardy geraniums, *Tiarella cordifolia* (foam flower) and other ground-cover plants have been added and have seeded and increased generously. The overall effect is really very charming, and virtually labour free. I planted a cutting of the very vigorous, gloriously orange-blossom-scented rambler rose, 'Wedding Day', at the foot of the walnut tree where it is rapidly romping upwards and before long will cascade down and overhang the patio, adding to the overall mid-summer perfumes, particularly in the evenings. I have often been woken on a hot summer's night by the scent of *Lilium regale* wafting up through the bedroom window. However, I learnt a lesson years ago never to be tempted to bring them into the house for flower arranging, as their perfume then really does become too much of a good thing, being overpoweringly sickly. Better to let it waft in on the night air through open doors and windows. All in all, I'm really very happy about our 'great wall of China' now.

Stone walls can be very effective in a garden and can be used in varied ways. They are so mellow and, regardless of how they are used, they are always such a compliment to perennials, trees and shrubs. Each year I find more situations where they can help enhance the general appearance of the garden layout

The small retaining wall built around this border at the back of the house helps contain both soil and moisture.

as well as being very practical. Over the years we have planted up new corners, adding compost and top soil to improve the general condition of the existing earth, but since these areas are raised up from, and slope down to, the paths and lawns, they tend to erode every time it rains. Several small retaining walls, which have been built at these sites, are a great success. Not only do they contain the soil and much more moisture, but they can be used to allow low-growing plants to drape over their sides, showing them off to best advantage, rather than collapsing in a heap and frequently destroying the grass underneath. This way too, contours are softened. We usually manage to find enough stone to build these walls, but finding soil to fill in behind them is more difficult. Virtually every square inch of this garden is planted up, and I have a real problem when I need to fill a garden tub or container with soil or top up a hole where I have dug something out. We have three fairly large compost heaps but they cannot cope with the demands of the whole garden, and I now wish I had reserved more space for them. I have often been tempted to buy one of the garden shredders that are available, to provide us with our own mulch.

The roses, particularly those on the pergola and the old-fashioned shrub varieties, generate the largest proportion of garden waste that cannot be composted, and I would hesitate to use the shredded prunings of roses on the garden for fear of spreading disease, particularly rust and blackspot. I prefer to burn all rose prunings. Blackspot is a real problem in the country with our relatively unpolluted air and it would be foolhardy consciously to spread the disease. There is nothing as forlorn-looking as a rose totally infected with it. Time permitting, in the summer I try to strip off all infected leaves before they fall and burn them. The plant may look somewhat naked for a while but soon produces fresh young leaves. Most of the roses covering our pergola are ramblers and they seem to be very disease prone, as are many of the old-fashioned shrub varieties, so we try to keep them sprayed on a weekly basis in the summer, and as a result they generally reward us by looking and smelling wonderful throughout the summer. However, I'm not so enthusiastic about the ramblers in late summer and autumn when they have finished flowering and require their annual hair-cut – they get a real short back and sides – as they are so thorny and lethal. By trial and error we have worked out the best way to tackle the problem, taking each rose down from its support, cutting out most of the old flowering wood at the base and then training the new young growth by winding it around the post on which, hopefully, it will flower the following year. Obviously you have to be a bit careful as the young growth is very tender and brittle. It looks awful when it is first done – very naked – and with this excuse I usually put off the pruning as long as possible, certainly until after our final official charity open days. One lesson I have learnt with the planting up of the pergola is not to

ABOVE *Bonfires are an ongoing event in our garden. Here Len burns infected rose prunings.*

RIGHT *Rambler, climbing and shrub roses growing up and alongside the pergola give a spectacular display in high summer but generate a prodigious amount of non-compostible waste at pruning time.*

interplant roses with honeysuckle or clematis that may require pruning at a different time of the year, because it is impossible to do one without damaging the other. Also, if you are allergic to rose thorns, don't plant roses on your trellis or pergola, unless you stick to the thornless varieties or you can get someone else to do the pruning for you.

Another definite 'don't' that I have learnt through bitter experience is don't create herbaceous borders under wild fruit trees. The wild plum trees we inherited provide a lovely feature in the garden and I was grateful to have at least some mature trees as a basis on which to build part of the framework of the garden. However I didn't take into account the prolific harvest of plums that these trees produce each year – no late frosts or biting north-east winds put them off, it seems. The spring blossom, always the first to arrive, is delightful, so dainty and welcome, but secretly my heart always sinks, thinking ahead to late summer, and I hope a frost will come along to prevent the fruit from setting. The reason for this is not because the fruit aren't absolutely delicious – even if we do have a freezer full of plums and enough plum jam to last for years – but because in my ignorance I created the herbaceous border under them on the south-facing side. When the plums ripen they come tumbling down in their hundreds in amongst all the plants, hiding and nestling secretly under leaves. Try as I do to pick them all up, I always miss countless numbers, with the result that the following year I find phlox, paeonies, delphiniums and other plants competing with a plum tree in the middle of their glory. The speed with which plum seedlings put their roots down to almost unfathomable depths almost suggests that they know they shouldn't be there and are determined to make it as difficult as possible to be uprooted. As if this wasn't enough they also produce endless suckers, which are not only very thirsty but have a great appetite, and so the ground in this area becomes somewhat starved. The most effective way I have found to deal with them is to place a cut-off plastic bottle over the offending youngster and then to spray down inside it with a systemic weedkiller or brushwood killer, thereby preventing any damage to surrounding plants. This has been the most difficult area in which to create an effective planting scheme, and I frequently experiment with different groupings. *Crambe cordifolia* never seems to mind how dry or starved it is and is ideally suited to these conditions. Its enormous size and architectural shape with huge rhubarb-like leaves and gigantic flower heads seem to belie this – to look at a crambe in its full-flowering glory you would be forgiven for thinking that here is a plant that would be very thirsty. The stunning gypsophila-like flower sprays, which stand anything up to 8 feet (2.5 m) above the crown of leaves, have a honey perfume. I leave the flowering stalks long after they have turned to seed heads as they are still attractive and being on such a massive scale can leave an unsightly gap once cut back.

Perfume and scent have an important role to play in a garden and we all have our own preferences. On the whole we tend to associate garden scents with long, hot summer days and nights and particularly with plants like roses, lilies and lavender. However there are others which are welcome long before many plants have even emerged from their winter sleep. The winter-flowering *Corylopsis pauciflora* can suddenly flood an area of the garden with its perfume in weak late-winter sunshine. The humble primrose has a gentle, haunting and, to me, nostalgic perfume and many winter and spring bulbs flower

The wild plum tree blossom is always a lovely and welcome sight in spring.

with their own distinctive sweet scents. In late spring the exquisite exochorda not only delights with its pure white blossom but its perfume hangs on the air all around it, as does that of the bird cherry (*Prunus padus*), with its racemes of white flowers like miniature wisteria blooms. Foliage, too, provides an enormous range of perfume. One of the few benefits of having to cut the lawn edges is the constant assault on my nostrils of delicious scents as I brush against low-growing plants – lavender, hyssop, rosemary, artemisia, and nepeta (catmint), to name but a few. There are some plants which need to be given a little encouragement to release their secret scent, by rubbing their leaves. *Houttuynia cordata* which has a strong Seville-orange perfume, is one; and with its very aromatic indefinable smell, the quiet gentle, almost retiring pale-yellow-flowered *Nepeta govaniana* is another. There are others which I don't like at all, one of them being rue (*Ruta graveolens*), which I would call a smell rather than a perfume and which clings to your clothes and hands long after you have been in contact with it. Many plants give off their best perfume at night for the benefit of moths. Honeysuckle is the most obvious one that comes to mind. We have one climbing the wall outside our bedroom window, and it's lovely in the summer both to go to sleep and wake to its gentle perfume. I don't know if lilies have any particular reason for being so highly scented at night other than waking you up to remind you that they are there, but I wouldn't be without them. One plant that keeps its secret most effectively is the glorious shrub *Elaeagnus angustifolia* 'Caspica'. Its glistening silver foliage is

reward enough, but it is also very generous with its perfume. The very pale, yellow flowers are so tiny and insignificant as to be almost unnoticeable, so that when their perfume pervades the air it is difficult to know where it is coming from.

There are perfumes in the garden which seem to be irresistible to cats. The most obvious is nepeta (catmint). As we have three cats I'm often asked how I manage to grow nepeta successfully and the only reason I can think of is that we have so much – great mounds of it at intervals down the pergola – that the cats have either got tired of it or the general scent of it everywhere to their highly sensitive nostrils is enough to satisfy them. However there is another plant that all of them have found totally irresistible, and that is the twining climber *Actinidia kolomikta* which grows up our garage. It is a fascinating plant with heart-shaped leaves splashed with cream and pink – almost as though someone had thrown a couple of tinfuls of paint over them. But it is even more fascinating to cats. It attracts them primarily in the spring when the sap is rising and the buds forming, and perhaps it exudes a powerful aroma which only cats can pick up, as I can't say I have noticed it. When I planted ours I feared for its survival as it was pulled and chewed and rubbed against – more than once I had to tuck it back into the ground and eventually had to provide it with a wire-netting cage to protect it. It is now well established and covering the garage, but each spring the cats are back at it again having a good rub and a nibble with silly grins on their faces. In fact the only time they show any real interest in the nepeta is in the spring when the young growth is emerging.

When crushed, the variegated leaves of Houttuynia cordata *'Chameleon' give off a scent of oranges.*

People who don't own cats often justifiably complain of the damage they do in their gardens, scratching up freshly tilled earth, newly planted seeds and seedlings and precious plants. I find the best deterrent to visiting cats is having my own cats, and to deter my cats from parts of the garden, I sometimes use wire netting bent into domes and placed over precious treasures until they can hold their own. Alternatively upended hanging baskets are ideal. It all looks a bit strange but is only necessary for a brief time in the spring, and once the borders begin to fill out the problem is more or less solved. Then the borders become daytime dormitories as our cats shelter under overhanging shrubs on hot days – frequently all three of them lying hidden within a few feet of each other.

Despite the cats we still have a lovely abundance of wildlife, although every now and then a rescue job is necessary. The hedgehogs, being nocturnal and having protective coats, are pretty safe. It's a delight in the spring when they announce their emergence from hibernation by leaving their little black-cigar 'visiting cards' around the garden. The frogs and birds are somewhat more vulnerable. Now and then there will be a high-pitched squeal followed by a 'plop' and a splash in the pond, as a frog goes flying through the air followed by a cat, trying to get through the undergrowth in hot pursuit. As far as I know only once has one of the cats actually fallen in. Elsewhere in the garden, escape is a bit more difficult for frogs although the densely planted borders provide a good degree of protection. If a cat does catch up with one of them, it never really seems to know what to do with it. More than once I have come across a somewhat bemused and disorientated frog in the kitchen.

We also have a large and varied collection of bird visitors brave enough to rear their young here. Of course there have been some casualties, but happily only a few. I suspect far more have fallen prey to magpies. Frequently in the early morning I hear distress calls from families of blackbirds trying to protect their nests and young, and fend off marauding magpies who raid the nests stealing eggs and young alike. The magpies in this part of the country appear to be reaching epidemic proportions. I suppose it is the law of the jungle but sometimes I wonder how long other birds will continue visiting and taking up residence in the garden. I only hope that, by providing the habitat and food and water, especially in winter, to attract the garden birds, they will be able to breed in sufficient numbers to counteract this threat. It would be a sad day indeed to be woken by a dawn chorus consisting solely of the unmusical 'tonk tonk' of the magpie.

I wonder how often and how many of us have said we haven't room for even one more plant in our gardens, but equally how many of us always manage to find that little space in which to squeeze that coveted treasure or, as usually happens with me, a whole new carload of plants. A couple of years ago I decided I would really like to have a mass of *Perovskia atriplicifolia*, the blue-flowered, silver-foliaged Russian sage, for late summer, but simply didn't have a suitable area that was large enough, so there was nothing for it but to create one. There was still a bit of lawn that I felt I could manage without, so this was dug out to a width of about 3 feet (1m) on the

The perfume of climbing roses wafts through the open bedroom windows in summer.

south-west-facing side of one of the small fences
enclosing the front garden. In order to give long-
term interest to this bed, rather than just having the
perovskia, which only flowers in late summer, I filled
it with an early-flowering white tulip, 'Purissima'
('White Emperor'), which never fails to come up
each year and increases quite rapidly – a very
rewarding variety both for the garden and for
picking for the house. Then it was a question of what
to have to follow on from this during early and mid
summer, so I decided to plant clumps of *Allium
aflatunense*, which has lovely deep-lilac grapefruit-
sized heads, together with *Lychnis coronaria oculata*,
the white variety with a pink eye. This I have found
to be an enormously worthy plant because if it is
deadheaded virtually daily throughout the summer,
it will go on flowering from early summer right
through to mid-autumn or the first frosts. It's always
worth collecting some seed as sometimes the plants
flower themselves to death. The blue-mauve spires
of the perovskia come up through the branching
lychnis in late summer. On the other side of the
fence is a bank of old-fashioned shrub roses which
flower predominantly in early summer and through
part of mid-summer. At their feet I have planted
several of the perennial white-flowered sweetpea,
Lathyrus latifolius albus, which sadly has no perfume,
but nonetheless is a glorious late-summer climber,
or more appropriately scrambler. They clamber into
the roses after they have finished flowering and been
cut back, thereby providing some interest on both
sides of the fence.

ABOVE (LEFT) *'Purissima' tulips, mass-planted along the fence
and in the garden in front of the cottage, make a lovely
display in spring.*

RIGHT *A 'hedge' of* Lychnis coronaria oculata *interplanted
with the late summer-flowering Russian sage,*
Perovskia atriplicifolia.

Under the perovskia and lychnis is *Artimisia schmidtiana*, a low, carpeting, fine-foliaged, intensely silver variety, which is non-invasive but increases rapidly enough to do its job of covering the ground. This is more effective if you prevent it from flowering by nipping off the little buds as they appear, otherwise it tends to get woody and 'leggy'. There are also a few clumps of the dainty *Parahebe catarractae alba*, another very useful plant with pretty, glossy, evergreen leaves and airy sprays of white flowers throughout the summer, which carpet, or rather, tumble gently over the edges of the border. I'm quite pleased with this flower bed because although it was so much an afterthought I tried to put into practice some of the things I have learnt over the last few years. Not only does it give long-term interest but its silvery, pale tones make quite an impact. I didn't set out to make it a white border as such, but these plants seem to revel in this particular situation, where they get full sun virtually all day long, and thereby give of their best and are more effective than had they to struggle against the odds. On a smaller scale I would imagine the perovskia on its own, underplanted with *Artemisia schmidtiana* would make a shining combination, and I may just have to consider doing this very soon. Having set out to provide a setting primarily for the perovskia – indeed to have a glorious mass planting of it – it has now been somewhat overtaken by the lychnis, which has well and truly stolen the limelight. The perovskia still grows happily through the lychnis but really doesn't have the starring role, as was intended. It looks as though another bit of lawn may have to be sacrificed, as I have become rather fond of my lychnis hedge.

ABOVE (RIGHT) *Shrub roses 'Fantin Latour' and 'Empress Josephine' on one side of the fence which encloses the front garden, with* Lychnis coronaria oculata *in the foreground.*

A lot of plants benefit from deadheading on a regular basis throughout the summer, for in most cases it prolongs the flowering life of the plant. However with a number of them I find it essential to leave on some seed heads at the end of the summer to allow the plants to seed naturally. Nature, in my experience, is a much better propagator than I can ever be – wildflowers and weeds bear witness to this. With this in mind I think it's worth emphasizing the need to take care when weeding and hoeing. In fact I never hoe – I don't like it and find it backbreaking. When I weed, it is a question of getting down on hands and knees or squatting, because as a 'hands and knees' gardener, I find I have more control. It's so easy to slice things off or damage wanted seedlings when wielding a hoe, and thus lose out on nature's 'freebies'.

It's very exciting discovering seedlings in the garden. You may not always immediately recognize what is what, but after a time you begin to learn to distinguish between a weed and a cultivated-plant seedling. When in doubt I leave well alone until it becomes obvious what something might be, or I pot it up and wait and see. Over the years I've grown a range of extraordinarily healthy specimens of weeds, which seemingly couldn't believe their luck in being treated to lovely rich potting compost instead of having to struggle through stony cracks and paths! There are numerous plants that I rely on for seedlings: *Lychnis coronaria*, campanulas, *Rosa glauca* (*R. rubrifolia*), violas, hellebores, linarias, lobelias and many more. The delightful *Omphaloides cappadocica*, with its starry, blue, forget-me-not flowers blooming from mid-spring until autumn, also seeds itself and in this garden tolerates very dry shade, which is so useful. The tiny maiden pink, *Dianthus deltoides*, and the little pink and white daisy, *Erigeron mucrona-*

tus, seed themselves merrily about in a rough stone path, and another very good seeder is the exquisitely beautiful *Verbena bonariensis*. I have it in amongst some of the old-fashioned shrub roses, because it flowers very late, long after the roses have gone over and been pruned hard. It grows very tall, with long, wiry, branching stems standing proud above the roses and neighbouring plants, which lend it support, and produces a haze of lilac for weeks on end in late summer right through into autumn, when the frosts arrive to tarnish the blooms. The parent plant may not always come through the winter, but you have no need to worry because once you've grown one you'll have thousands more. The seedlings first appear in early summer as tiny little specks dotted around in flower beds and paths, and by late summer or early autumn they will have reached full-grown flowering-sized plants of 4 to 5 feet (1.2–1.5 m) tall. It is quite amazing how rapidly they grow.

The miniature spring- and autumn-flowering cyclamen are also great seeders and thereby increase rapidly, which is most rewarding. They are charming additions to any garden and always such a welcome surprise, appearing almost without warning, unfolding their dainty little heads quite unexpectedly before their leaves arrive on the scene. These, too, have a significant role to play, with their variety of shape and colouring, forming a carpet of glossy, often exquisitely marbled foliage. In the case of the late summer- and autumn-flowering varieties, the leaves remain fresh and attractive right through the winter and on into late spring, when they die back, allowing the corm to rest and gather its strength for the next performance. I remember, one autumn, visiting a small château on the Loire in France, which belongs to the family of some French friends of ours, where there were carpets of cyclamen growing in

Regular deadheading of Lychnis coronaria oculata *prolongs its flowering life.*

Late summer- and autumn-flowering Cyclamen hederifolium *are prolific seeders and will carpet an area in a relatively short time.*

the park. It was an amazing sight with sheets of pink and white as far as the eye could see, with scarcely room to put your feet down in between the flowers. There was no garden, just a scruffy patch of grass in the middle of the drive approaching the château, and the cyclamen had been allowed to run riot for years, providing an unforgettable memory for anyone who saw them. Seedlings such as these are all part of nature's generosity and so often she deposits them in just the right place. Frequently a plant has appeared in my garden, where it would never have occurred to me to put it or indeed where I would not have been able to squeeze it in, and it looks perfect in its

setting. However there are times, of course, when plants can look, and be, very awkward. My supposedly weed-free gravel paths are in fact a most successful medium for germinating seeds and I have come to rely on their produce for quite a number of plants each year.

A densely planted – or indeed an overplanted – garden, as mine is, can create problems, and true to say I have lost a number of plants due to their being swamped. But it also helps to minimize other problems and certainly weeds have less chance of getting a hold. When I can eventually get into the borders in the autumn and winter to cut back and tidy up generally, I find that the weeds are usually fairly spindly, weak creatures and are easily rooted out. However, I have learnt by experience that creating a full and natural effect and ensuring continuity by dense planting does require management. It doesn't happen simply by stuffing in plants at random until there are no gaps and letting them get on with it. Many a time I have wished I could say to a shrub or tree: 'Stop right here, you're just the right size now. Please don't grow any more!' Sadly that doesn't work, so I'm learning through trial and error the value of judicial pruning.

As well as the roses, especially those on the pergola, and the old-fashioned shrub varieties, there are many other shrubs that I find I can contain with, and actually benefit from, hard pruning and are consequently so much easier to manage. As a general rule the spring- and early summer-flowering shrubs I prune hard after they have flowered, removing most of the old, flowering wood low down and leaving the young growth on which it will bloom the following year. However, as always, there are exceptions: for example I cut lavender and sage hard in the spring, before rather than after flowering. Both of these get very woody and tatty, and this hard pruning encourages young growth, keeps them fresh and compact , and reduces the need to replace them so frequently. There are others to which I give a very short hair-cut in the spring. I find *Spiraea japonica* 'Goldflame' benefits from a severe cut-back as it is about to burst into leaf. Not only does it keep it from getting leggy but the young fresh growth emerges a wonderful copper colour. I prune it again later on, sometimes more than once in the summer, to prevent it from flowering, as I prefer to have just the gold foliage. *Physocarpus opulifolius* 'Luteus', which has peeling bark and dainty golden foliage in spring, also benefits from a hard prune early on before coming into leaf, as does *Viburnum opulus* 'Aureum'. Both of

these are very vigorous and, as I have limited space, they need to be contained to a certain extent. So much depends on what is required of a shrub. If you have the space to give them their head and grow enormous, and that is what you want, then with many of them you can let them go. I have found though that most deciduous shrubs benefit from having weak and old flowering wood removed for the general health, well-being and appearance of the plant.

By mid-summer a lot of herbaceous perennials are beginning to look tired and worn out and these too, frequently reward you with a second showing if hard pruned. The catmint, *Viola cornuta* and delphiniums growing alongside the pergola path all get cut back to the ground in mid-summer and recover again into new growth. We usually have a second blooming of delphiniums in the autumn, and the catmint and violas start reflowering from late summer, often until Christmas.

The expression 'the June gap' relating to British gardens, suggests there is a lull between spring- and early-summer-performing plants but here I have found there is far more of a mid-summer 'July gap', which has proved more difficult to fill. Admittedly the shrub roses are usually still giving a lovely show, if there hasn't been too much rain to damage their blooms, but the herbaceous borders are showing signs of deterioration. The delphiniums, poppies and lupins have been cut back and the paeonies, irises and many of the campanulas have passed their best, as have many of the flowering shrubs and trees. At the same time many other perennials have yet to produce their summer show. So it's worth looking out for plants that give long-term interest in terms of either flowers or foliage, to help cover this gap. I've already mentioned some plants that fill this role, notably *Lychnis coronaria* and *Campanula persicifolia*, which bloom throughout the summer months, but there are many others like the tradescantias, some of the euphorbias and malvas, *Dicentra formosa* varieties, hostas and ferns, which provide interest. Summer-flowering bulbs also have a significant role to play in mid-summer, particularly lilies, allium and brodiaea.

From mid-summer the borders can begin to look blowzy and overblown and even messy in places. This is when I begin to feel dissatisfied and become most aware of my mistakes in planting schemes. I long to start moving things around. In fact I often do, and although it may set the plants back for a while, they always pick up fairly quickly, provided I don't disturb the roots and make sure they are well watered and supported where necessary after transplanting. Once I see what I consider to be a glaring mistake in a planting scheme it bothers me and I can't rest until I can rectify it. I also find it more

RIGHT *Electric scarlet phlox 'Starfire', lythrum, echinacea, eryngium and purple-leaved sage all contribute to a spectacular display in a late summer border.*

BELOW Allium albopilosum *and* A. azureum *interplanted with* Scabiosa *'Butterfly Blue',* Linum perenne, *the glaucous blue leaves of* Mertensia asiaticum *and* Dianthus deltoides.

difficult to site a plant in exactly the right place when it is cut back in the autumn or winter and I cannot actually see it growing in relation to its neighbours. Even a few inches out can make all the difference to the balance of the whole grouping of plants.

With the arrival of late summer, suddenly the garden is full of promise again. The phlox, *Eryngium* (sea-hollies), agapanthus, *Lythrum* (purple loose-strife), perennial lobelias, *Thalictrum dipterocarpum* and Japanese anemones all begin to take over from the earlier perennials, and the delphiniums, violas, nepeta, floribunda and hybrid tea roses are all taking on a new lease of life ready for a second helping of bloom, with many others waiting in the wings. Suddenly the garden is a blaze of colour again, helped by the almost overnight ripening of rose hips. I love the late-summer and early-autumn garden. There is such a wealth of flowers in these months with many rich and regal colours as well as soft pastel ones. It is relatively easy to have a pretty spring garden or indeed a lovely early-summer one, and it may initially be more difficult to plan for late summer and autumn, as it requires thinking further ahead, but if you can achieve it the rewards are enormous.

In late autumn I start clearing my borders and getting them ready to put to bed for the winter. Some people prefer to leave the bulk of cutting back of herbaceous plants to the spring to provide protection against frosts and seeds for the birds, but I like to get most of it done during the late-autumn and winter months. The spring is such a busy time in the garden in many other aspects that I'm sure I would never get everything done then; also I feel that there is no reason for everywhere to be looking a mess, just because it is winter and I may not be spending much time outside. After all I can still see the garden from the house. It's easier too to distribute the rotted compost heaps and to apply manure and mulch to the border when they are relatively clear. Certainly some plants are best left to the spring before they are cut back – fuchsias, sedum and nepeta, among others – but I try to get most of the tidying-up and clearing done before the end of the winter, with the rubbish out of the way and burnt. Then with the first promise of spring, everything is ready for another year of anticipation and excitement.

Continuity of flowering is one of the most difficult things to achieve when planning a garden. One way to help achieve it is to buy plants in bloom at intervals on a regular basis throughout the year. By doing this, you will inevitably in future years always have something flowering throughout the seasons. However, there is rather more to it than just that. Thought has to go into what you'll plant next to or near something that might dominate an area for a relatively short time, but which then could leave an unsightly gap. Planting mixed borders of shrubs, trees and herbaceous perennials is one of the best ways of overcoming this. You can place the plants between the shrubs and trees which will continue to give shape and interest once the herbaceous plant has finished blooming. Bulbs can be easily planted in and amongst other plants, ground cover can be used to provide interest at a low level, and climbers like clematis and perennial sweetpeas can scramble up into shrubs and trees. Plants that have attractive foliage have the added bonus of giving interest both before and after flowering. The miniature cyclamen is a perfect example of this, and with the different varieties interplanted you can have almost all-the-year-round coverage of either flowers or foliage.

I often think that gardening has many parallels with cooking, especially preparing a gourmet meal. They share the same requirements of planning, thought, imagination and careful use of colour. Timing, presentation and continuity are of paramount importance, too, for you certainly don't want to have to sit and wait for lengthy periods between courses. So it is with gardening – to enjoy a garden to the full you need to have all the courses in terms of seasonal display from the appetizers through to the coffee, liqueurs and petits fours. Equally when you sit down to a special meal you enjoy it all the more with clean table linen, candles and all the trimmings. In a garden the distractions of weeds and disease can spoil the full flavour. To be a good cook I believe you have to enjoy good food and also enjoy preparing it. When making a meal or a garden, if it is a chore, the results will reflect this. You don't have to be expert, for we can all get guidance and help from the professionals and from books and friends, but it is important to keep experimenting and improvising, which I do both in the kitchen and the garden. Sometimes the results are sheer disaster but more often they are exciting and rewarding.

Half the fun of a garden is that there's always something new – a plant, a colour scheme to be explored, an established area to be redesigned, or a new one to be created. But nature is a great leveller. Sometimes when I am feeling quite pleased with myself because the garden is looking particularly good, along comes a torrential downpour of rain, often accompanied by high winds, which flatten everything; or a long drought in the summer, which

The garden takes on a different beauty in winter, particularly when covered in a thick blanket of snow.

makes everything look weary and sad; or devastating frosts in the winter, which kill off tender or young unestablished plants; and at any time of the year severe gales as well as many of nature's four- or more-legged friends can cause damage. They all play their part in making sure I don't get complacent. Then, just when I am on the point of despairing, nature sends along a great big bonus in one form or another, something I didn't expect – perhaps a flower blooming with unusual exuberance, a treasure which I had thought lost and is now reappearing with renewed vigour, extra seedlings, or more spectacular autumn colouring than usual. Nature is totally fair as she is totally unselective. It doesn't matter whether you own a large country estate with a fleet of gardeners or a humble little plot: we all suffer from the elements but also reap their rich rewards. Usually we keep at it and don't give up, thinking next year it will all be better.

One of the greatest rewards of having a garden is knowing that its attending joys, excitements and beauty are for life. Recently someone quoted to me:

'If you want to be happy for a few hours, get drunk; if you want to be happy for a few years, get married; but if you want to be happy for life, get a garden.' The first two comments are perhaps somewhat cynical, but I would certainly concur with the last. The happiness derived from a garden is not a short-lived 'one off'. If the winter is devastating, you know that spring must follow, with so much to look forward to in the months ahead, and even if the summer is disappointing, God willing, there is always next year, when everything must surely be better and when there will be new things to do, new plants to discover and grow, and the acquaintance of old friends to be renewed. For gardeners there is no peace to compare with that found in their gardens. It's hard work but totally relaxing, it's disappointing but joyful, and above all it's mysterious, magical and miraculous. A little word of warning, though, from one victim – it can become a passion. But it's one that I consider myself very blessed to have, together with the opportunity to indulge it.

DESIGN
– AND –
PLANTING

THE FRONT GARDEN

Access to the front garden from the road west of the cottage is gained by a five-bar gate into a driveway. A gravel path, over which the pergola was constructed, has replaced the original narrow strip of tarmac and extends in a straight line about two thirds of the way down the garden. Wide, curved borders, densely planted with trees, shrubs, bulbs and herbaceous perennials, surround the lawns on either side of the pergola.

In the lawn on the north side of the pergola a small orchard has been created with a selection of fruit trees underplanted with spring bulbs. The old apple tree in the lawn on the south side of the pergola is underplanted with spring bulbs, pulmonarias and alchemilla, ensuring all-year-round interest and cover.

At the end of the pergola the path winds in a gentle curve to the front door, where pink lavender borders the path along the front of the cottage. Here a post and rail fence encloses smaller separate areas, which differ considerably from each other and from the larger ones beyond. Shrub roses predominate, and this area close to the house is richly scented in high summer with the perfume from lilies, roses and lavender.

A weeping ornamental pear tree in the lawn to the left of the path is underplanted with tulips and autumn-flowering cyclamen; and a large beech tree, which overhangs the south boundary border, is underplanted with shrubs, spring bulbs, and shade-tolerant ground-cover plants.

Through the Pergola

The pergola, constructed from tanalized timber, straddles the straight line of the gravelled path which leads to the cottage. Openings on both sides, over the scalloped beds running down its length, allow access to the separate gardens created on either side.

One of the few visions I had of the garden at the outset was of a tunnel of blues and misty purples which would carry the eye through and give a feeling of mystery as to what lay at the far end. This vision has been achieved in high summer by clothing the framework of the pergola in roses, clematis and honeysuckle; by underplanting with nepeta, blue and white *Viola cornuta* and *Anthemis punctata* ssp. *cupaniana* along the borders of the path; and by planting clumps of delphiniums and shrub roses to create the walls of the tunnel. An intense tapestry of soft cool pastel shades is produced, enhanced by a wonderful pot pourri of perfumes.

The pergola takes on a different personality according to the season and the changing planting schemes in the borders on either side. In spring tulips line the path, and in late summer Japanese anemone hybrids replace the earlier-flowering delphiniums, while the violas continue to bloom right through into winter, alongside the silver foliage and papery flowers of *Anaphalis triplinervis*.

The climbing rose 'Bantry Bay' on one of the pergola supports with shrub roses, delphiniums and Viola cornuta.

Early spring
In winter and early spring the bare bones of the pergola show the evidence of the severe pruning of the roses in the previous autumn; and there is a clear view down the length of the path before the roses and herbaceous plants stir from their winter sleep.

Mid-spring
Half way through the spring the tulips have started to bloom and the nepeta, in woolly clumps at intervals along the path, has taken on its fresh young growth. Spring has definitely arrived with the blooming of a *Clematis macropetala* among the rambler roses, which are just beginning to stir.

Late spring
All the promise of summer is evident by late spring. Violas and anthemis have already started flowering, and nepeta is about to burst into bloom. The rambler and shrub roses are in full leaf and heavy with bud in readiness for their starring performance in a few weeks time.

Early summer
Throughout the early summer months the pergola reaches its peak with the roses competing for first prize, floating above the misty, mauve haze of nepeta and violas at their feet. Clumps of stately delphinium spires stand sentinel at intervals in the beds bordering the gravel path.

BY THE COTTAGE

The garden at the end of the pergola immediately in front of the cottage, is separated from the main area of the front garden by a post and rail fence which is planted up with a variety of shrub roses. It is divided into two by the final stretch of the path, which takes on a gentle curve to the front door. In spring white flowers dominate this garden with mass plantings of tulip 'Purissima' ('White Emperor') and narcissus 'Thalia' and with the flowering Japanese cherries. In summer roses are the main theme, and their perfumes mingle with those of the lavender and lilies bordering the paths and the honeysuckle growing against the cottage.

Silver-leaved *Pyrus salicifolia* 'Pendula' in the lawn on one side of the path is underplanted with *Cyclamen hederifolium* for autumn and winter interest, and clumps of blue-leaved hostas carpet the ground at the feet of the shrub roses along the fence.

A large beech tree overhanging the lawn on the other side of the path creates a cool, shady area for sitting on hot summer days. Here I have planted mainly shade-tolerant shrubs and ground-cover plants, together with a variety of spring bulbs. Dicentras take over from the white tulips under the shrub roses along the fence, and repeat-flowering musk roses fill a bed bordering the path.

In mid-summer roses are blooming everywhere, especially at the front of the cottage, where they border paths and fences and clothe the walls in the company of honeysuckle.

Early spring
An upstairs window gives a clear view up the garden in winter. Miniature daffodils, crocuses and emerging tulip leaves are the first signs of life in an otherwise bare landscape, and announce the imminent arrival of spring.

Mid-spring
Japanese cherries, 'Purissima' tulips and 'Thalia' narcissi provide a dazzling display of white flowers over several weeks, highlighted by the unfurling, young, silver foliage of *Pyrus salicifolia* 'Pendula'.

Mid-summer
In summer shrub roses along the fence come into their full glory, with hosta leaves unfurled at their feet. Lilies along the path are ready to burst into bloom and *Pyrus salicifolia* 'Pendula' shimmers in full sun. At night honeysuckle perfumes the air.

Early spring
Miniature narcissi are the first signs of life in the winter landscape seen from under the beech tree. Soon other spring bulbs will follow, together with young spring foliage, the dainty flowers of epimediums and unfurling hosta leaves.

Mid-spring
Fresh young foliage begins to cover the bare earth under the beech tree. *Fritillaria meleagris*, erythroniums, narcissi, hyacinths and primulas are joined by emerging hostas and epimediums, and hydrangeas start to burst into new life, while in the background the spring garden is already well advanced.

Late spring
The lush young foliage of trees, shrubs and ground-cover plants creates an area of many different hues of green in the dappled shade under the beech tree, giving a wonderful feeling of peace, tranquillity and coolness on hot days.

Late summer
Hydrangea blooms begin to light up the more densely shaded area created by the overhanging branches of the beech tree in full leaf. They will linger on defiantly through the winter, fading gracefully and taking on shades of shot silk, before finally retiring.

Early spring
In early spring the skeletal form of the pergola stands out nakedly. Cyclamineus narcissi, also visible from the house, are bravely blooming to lift the spirits. Elsewhere other spring bulbs are pushing through the bare earth, and trees and shrubs are beginning to bud up in anticipation of warmer days to come.

Mid-spring
After a long dreary winter, nothing is lovelier than a garden in spring with breathtaking, foamy blossom and a wide range of bulbs and foliage. Everything emerges fresh and pristine, and the excitement of more to come in the months ahead is worth all the waiting.

Late spring
By late spring everything is lush and rich in texture and colour. Roses on the pergola and along the fence are ready to burst into flower; euphorbias, anthemis and dicentras are already blooming; and the young beetroot-coloured foliage of *Heuchera micrantha* 'Palace Purple' has emerged.

Mid-summer
The cottage is almost obscured from view in summer when the roses are in full bloom and the trees clad in their summer foliage. Roses are the stars at this time of the year, but many other perennials shine and make their own contribution to the overall picture.

THE BACK GARDEN

The garden to the rear of the cottage is divided into three distinctive areas. Two of them are made up of mixed borders, lawns and paved areas for sitting and having meals, and are on two levels. A low, curved dry-stone wall, constructed to support the raised area, divides the two levels. Below it a rough stone path borders the grass running around a kidney-shaped island bed in the lawn.

There are large, curved borders on two sides of this lawn and a paved sitting area immediately outside the house. Two sets of shallow steps lead up through the low wall to the higher level. Here a bed is planted with a mixture of hybrid tea and floribunda roses with tulips in the spring and lilies in summer. A narrow bed along the top of the wall is planted with roses and alpines. A small patio under a walnut tree is sited in the corner of the lawn and overlooks the field. On the north-facing boundary trees and shrubs are underplanted with hellebores, spring bulbs and ground-cover plants.

A paved path all around the back of the cottage links the sitting area outside the kitchen door with the paths in the front garden. A narrow, stone path under an arch cuts through the borders on the lower level into a small, secluded, round garden, where encircling trees and shrubs are underplanted with spring flowers and foliage plants. Nearby the little pond, surrounded by hostas, ferns and irises, nestles under the plum trees and is approached from another area of the garden by a gravel path.

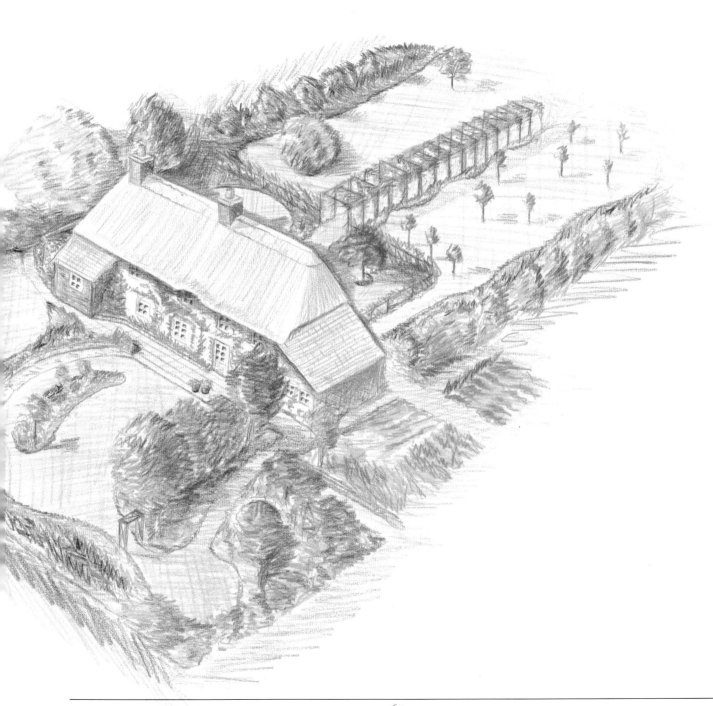

THE SPLIT LEVEL GARDEN

The area of garden to the rear and south-east of the cottage occupies about two-thirds of the whole of the back garden. Its layout, on two levels, has created two distinctive areas which are divided by a low dry-stone wall supporting the higher level. An illusion of a shallow sunken garden has been created in the lower level by the addition of another similar wall on the other side enclosing a curved south-facing border, backed by a line of wild plum trees. Another wide border on the boundary with the fields is planted up with a variety of trees, shrubs and herbaceous perennials, and a kidney-shaped island bed is sited off centre in the lawn. The curved and rounded edges of all the beds here give flowing movement to the overall design.

On the raised level a bed running along the top of the wall opens out into a larger border and is planted with a mixture of roses, alpines, spring bulbs and lilies. The patio which was constructed in one corner makes an ideal position for barbecues on summer evenings, and another shady bed under trees on the north-facing side is filled with shrubs, bulbs, hellebores and ground-cover plants. A paved path round the house gives access to the front garden on both sides.

Ethereal sprays of honey-scented Crambe cordifolia *arch above the long-flowering shrub rose 'Louise Odier' and, together with blue and white* Campanula persicifolia, *make an effective group planting on the corner of a border.*

Early spring

A border backed by wild plum trees separates the pond and round garden from the main area of the back garden. A small retaining wall around it helps to contain the moisture and prevent soil erosion. In early spring, bulbs and herbaceous perennials begin to emerge from winter dormancy.

Early summer

Once the trees have come into leaf, the pond is no longer visible from the house. The herbaceous border begins to fill out substantially early in the summer, and tall spires of delphiniums, with paeonies and roses, are about to burst into bloom.

Mid-summer

A mixture of roses, delphiniums and campanulas is the dominant feature of this bed in high summer, while a cloud of gypsophila-like *Crambe cordifolia* blooms makes a statement at the far end and low-growing plants drape themselves over the stone wall.

Early spring (opposite top)
Lovely *Helleborus orientalis* is the main feature of this area around the pond early in the year, with pulmonarias and dwarf rhododendrons. Here evergreen fronds of polystichums also provide shape and texture throughout the winter and spring months.

Mid-spring (left)
Spring is the one time of the year when flowers predominate in this area around the pond. Caltha thrives in the pond margin; narcissi, hellebores, pulmonarias and sedum all bloom happily together, as well as the exquisite pink and white forms of the aptly named *Dicentra spectabilis*. Young camellias are slowly establishing themselves.

Early summer (opposite bottom)
In summer the spring flowers around the pond give way to foliage plants. A variety of shape and texture provides interest for several months from hereon. Foamy lime-green flowers of alchemilla highlight the different shades of blue and green, and iris, hosta and hellebore leaves all jostle together, giving complete ground cover.

Early spring
Viewed from above, the contours and shapes of the back garden borders and lawn become most apparent in winter and early spring, before the dense planting blurs and softens edges and lines. However, even in a relatively bare landscape, stark shapes and outlines can create a beauty of their own.

Late spring
The borders in the back garden are planted to give as much long-term interest as possible. Shrubs and herbaceous perennials perform until late autumn, and most of the spring interest is created with differing foliage, noticeably that of a number of *Rosa glauca*.

Early summer
Shrub roses are once again a feature in this area of the garden in summer and are accompanied by different campanulas, hardy geraniums, scabious, delphiniums and many other herbaceous perennials in a medley of blue, pink, white, lilac and mauve.

The Pond and the Round Garden

The pond and little round garden alongside it make up a tiny, secret garden within the back garden, particularly secluded in summer when it is all but cut off by the trees that surround it. Access to it can be gained through a narrow arch leading from the main areas of the back garden or by a path alongside the pond. This is almost obscured in summer by clouds of alchemilla. Shrubs around the little circular lawn include *Viburnum burkwoodii*, exochorda and white lilac, all of which are sweetly scented with perfumes which hang on the air in the enclosed area.

This is essentially a foliage garden, but in winter clumps of *Helleborus orientalis* flowers bring it to life and are followed in spring by bulbs, *Dicentra spectabilis* and pulmonarias. In summer understated pools of colour are created by geraniums and violas amongst the hostas, irises, ferns and grasses, while a wild euphorbia seeds itself around and produces airy sprays of lime-green flowers for months on end, echoing the alchemilla.

Although very small, the pond is home to numerous frogs, and the birds and dragonflies appear grateful for its existence. In summer particularly, this is a very quiet, contemplative place and my favourite corner in the garden.

A gravel path alongside the pond, flanked by alchemilla, leads down to the little round garden. In early summer geraniums and violas provide a splash of colour in an otherwise green-toned foliage garden.

Early spring

The pond is clearly visible in spring before the surrounding plants have grown up to obscure it. Clumps of *Helleborus orientalis* are establishing themselves and give a lovely display through late winter, until later spring-flowering bulbs and plants come into bloom.

Mid-spring

Caltha enjoy a damp position in the pond margin; elsewhere narcissi, pulmonarias and *Dicentra spectabilis* begin to bring this part of the garden to life after the winter, and the trees get dressed in their spring green and blossom.

Early summer

Hostas, irises and alchemilla have taken over from the display of spring flowers, covering up the dead tatty leaves of earlier-flowering bulbs, and will continue to give long-term architectural and textural interest for several months. Flame-coloured *Euphorbia griffithii* 'Fireglow' blooms well in a dry spot under the trees.

Late summer

The green theme persists throughout the summer into autumn. Although there are very few flowers by late summer, colour is certainly not lacking, thanks to the variety of blue and green tones in the many foliage plants surrounding the pond.

Early spring
Clumps of *Helleborus orientalis* light up the area near the pond in the round garden as winter draws to a close. Evergreen ferns and russet-brown stems of *Stephanandra incisa* have provided interest in the winter months and spring bulbs have now pushed up their buds.

Mid-spring
As trees and shrubs begin to show off their spring green and blossom, spring bulbs and dicentras join with *Helleborus orientalis* to put on a lovely show before foliage plants unfurl their leaves and clothe the area in summer.

Late spring
With summer only just round the corner hostas have unfurled their wonderful textured and sculpted leaves, making a dramatic impact with their colour and form and performing the useful task of hiding old daffodil leaves. Candelabra primulas stand up in striking contrast.

Mid-summer
Lime-green sprays of alchemilla have burst onto the scene in full flower, contrasting beautifully with the rounded, ridged, blue leaves of *Hosta sieboldiana* while reflecting the yellow splashes in those of *Hosta fortunei* var. *albopicta*. Spikes of nectaroscordum rise up behind.

THE GARDEN
– IN THE –
HOUSE

This chapter is not, as the title might suggest, about houseplants, but about the different ways I use the garden inside the house. The most obvious is as a constant source of material for flower arrangements; the garden also provides pleasant views, framed by the windows, which we enjoy from inside the house; but its third role is of a more practical nature, because I have found it very helpful when making plans for the garden to get overall views from upstairs. Most of our borders have curved or wavy edges, and frequently it has proved difficult to get the line exactly right from ground level. I may sometimes spend hours running up and down the stairs trying to work out a shape, cutting away a bit each time until I feel I have got it right. I frequently fail to do so and have to spend yet more time rectifying the rectification! Who ever said that gardening was a relaxing hobby? However, it's much easier to get the correct balance and proportions by doing it this way, even if sometimes I end up with rather less lawn than I originally intended. Viewing the overall scene from above can also help with the planting and colour schemes, rather like standing back from a large painting to get a better idea of the whole picture.

As Ashtree Cottage is thatched, the upstairs windows are set very low and have deep sills where I can sit and ponder on shapes and colour schemes when trying to get new ideas or change a particular area that I may not be happy with. Also I have a lovely view from my bed when enjoying an early morning cup of tea. In the summer at first light I watch the birds looking for their breakfast, or having their baths in one of the bird-baths dotted around the garden. During these periods of quiet meditation I frequently get new ideas for the parts of the garden that I can see from there. Looking at the garden from this level gave me the idea to build another of the small retaining walls around one of the borders to the rear of the cottage. It matches up in line and height with the low dry-stone wall which had been constructed early on to divide the two levels and creates the impression of a shallow sunken garden quite separate from the areas on either side. Dividing the garden into different compartments has not only made it feel larger than it actually is, but has also provided much more interest. Different levels, paths running through borders, and planting schemes creating corners that draw you through into separate areas ensure that, rather than feasting your eyes on just one lovely picture, you travel on a journey of exploration around the garden and enjoy little gardens within the whole, each with its own personality and character.

I was able to fix the line of the path leading to the front door and the overall shape of the garden

In the summer, roses, delphiniums and nepeta provide a rich source of material for flower arranging.

immediately in front of the cottage by using the upstairs front windows. It was important to get the path just right, as it would not have been as easy to change as a flower bed. Sometimes an elevated position also gives a better overall view of how light and shade affect different parts of the garden at different times of the day. This is useful when deciding on planting schemes. Of course you can't always see all of the garden from the house, but assuming that it is possible and practical, it can be very helpful to use what I call 'the upstairs window technique.'

We are fortunate here in that the cottage is totally surrounded by the garden, so no matter which window we look out of we have a framed view of it. Even in the years when we have a glorious summer, we all, of necessity, have to spend a lot of our time inside. I don't think any passionate gardeners can enjoy any form of housework, as they always want to spend every spare minute of their time in their gardens, but we can all enjoy our gardens even when not actually in them. It's important to think of them as being an extension of our homes, and it's worth giving a little extra thought to the areas that you can see immediately from the windows, especially during the winter months. It doesn't matter whether it is a window box, a small courtyard, or something on a much grander scale.

We have a window at the top of our stairs, which provides a lovely view, particularly in spring when the two Japanese flowering cherry trees are in bloom. Their spreading branches make a canopy of snow-white blossoms at eye level as you go upstairs. Then in the summer months you can see along the top of the pergola where the predominance of the rose blooms amass, reaching for the sun, in a woven tapestry of creams, pinks and grape-purples. Downstairs there is a window that looks straight along the pergola at ground level, where the path is lined with the waving stems of the pink tulip 'Rosy Wings' in the spring. The picture changes to a haze of misty blues and mauves as the *Viola cornuta* and the nepeta take over in the summer.

An enormous *Rosa glauca* dominates a corner of the path running round the back of the house, its branches almost reaching into the bedroom window. This is a lovely picture all the year round and itself frames other views of the garden. In the winter the small birds feast off the hips still hanging on the branches, and the blackbirds scratch around underneath availing themselves of an easy meal on the carpet of fallen fruit. Roses growing all over the cottage perfectly frame views of the garden from all the windows in summer, often almost blocking out the daylight in their exuberance.

In late winter and early spring we can enjoy the arrival of the first snowdrops and crocuses, followed by some of the miniature narcissi. I planted these near the house so that we could see them on cold miserable days without having to venture out.

ABOVE *The prolific-flowering climbing rose 'Ballerina' clambers through the kitchen window.*

RIGHT *The lovely tulip 'Rosy Wings' lines the path under the pergola. These give way to 'Purissima' tulips, also called 'White Emperor', which are amassed along the fence further down.*

Throughout the summer months there is a never-ending succession of colour and shape of flowers and foliage. In early summer the predominance may be of blues, mauves and soft yellows, while in mid-summer this turns to pink and white roses and lilies before late summer moves on to a medley of different hues, including hot colours, announcing the imminent arrival of autumn just round the corner.

With the onset of autumn the fruit on the trees, most notably the crab apples and the rose hips, are already glowing, and the trees and shrubs have started to defoliate in places, allowing a longer and wider overall view of the garden. Some of the trees put on a last defiant display of brilliant colours before retiring gracefully to bed for the winter. The two stars in this final act of the year's show are the liquidambar and *Cornus nuttallii*, both of which put on a spectacular performance.

In the winter months the few conifers that I grow, evergreen shrubs and trees, hellebores, ferns and other evergreen plants, still provide a show of life in the garden together with hips and crab apples often lingering on right through the worst months. Some trees and shrubs give interest and shape with bark textures and colours, and architectural forms ensure there is always something to enjoy from inside the house.

If I cannot be outside I love to be able to gaze out of the windows all the year round, but one of my favourite views of the garden is through the open kitchen door. Sitting at my kitchen table I look out into the rear garden, with a view of one of the main borders. Our kitchen door is rarely closed during the day from the moment the central heating is turned off in the spring or early summer until the last possible moment in the autumn. Windows and doors allow the garden to be brought visually into the home, and we should capitalize on that.

Bringing some of the garden physically into the house can be achieved by using its wealth of colour, perfume and texture all the year round. One memory of my childhood and growing up is of a house which was never without flowers. Whether returning home for school holidays or later on for weekends away from working in London, I always found in my room a little vase of something picked from the garden by my mother. She had a great love of flowers and the house was always full of them, particularly in the summer months when every room was filled with the scent of roses and sweetpeas. I love the distinctive, all-pervading perfume of sweetpeas, which is sweet without being sickly, heady and yet somehow refreshingly light. No perfume maker even comes close to reproducing it.

It's lovely to be able to use some of the flowers and foliage from my garden in the house, sometimes backing them up with others that I've bought. It's sad that hellebores don't do well when cut and brought inside, as they would be among the first flowers to be picked for arranging at the turn of the year. However there is plenty to find for arrangements in winter, particularly foliage, the most obvious being sprigs of holly and ivy at Christmastime. I haven't yet planted any winter flowering jasmine – a fact I regret every winter as it is most attractive in any winter flower arrangement. I have to admit I don't really like forsythia and wouldn't normally grow it but for the fact that one of the very few things that greeted us when we arrived at Ashtree Cottage was a rather tragic-looking specimen, which I couldn't bring myself to throw out.

The view through the ever-open kitchen door where Panda inspects the latest harvest of deadheads in the trug.

However it is useful to pick in the depths of winter and bring into the house for forcing or mixing either with early daffodils from the Scilly Isles that arrive in the shops around Christmastime or with sprays of evergreen from the garden. A little later I do the same thing with sprays of ribes, the common red-flowering currant, and with amelanchier which, as its name – snowy mespulis – implies, has white blossom. Lovely as all the early, forced spring bulbs, like hyacinths and daffodils, are in their containers, it's nice to be able to have a vase of fresh flowers about the house in the depths of winter.

One of the most exciting moments in late winter is when I can pick that first tiny posy of snowdrops, cyclamen and violets, or any other little treasures that may appear shyly in the garden. Primroses and their colourful cousins have a habit of producing flowers at unexpected times and you can add them to miniature flower arrangements. Nowadays we are

RIGHT *One of my favourite narcissi, the pink-tinged 'Mrs R. O. Backhouse', is lovely both naturalized in the garden and in flower arrangements in the house.*

BELOW *The early flowering* Narcissus cyclamineus *'Tête-à-tête' blooms for weeks on end and is one of the first harbingers of spring.*

all being encouraged not to pick wild flowers as so many of them are in danger of disappearing from the countryside due to their shrinking habitat, but I remember as children we used to pick baskets full of primroses, made up in posies with a ruff of leaves tied up with pieces of wool, in the way the gypsies did when they sold them in the villages. We had large shallow bowls of them everywhere in the house around Eastertime. They have a quiet, soft perfume, which perfectly matches their gentle colouring and texture. It's sad that so many areas where they used to carpet the ground have now given way to concrete verges, housing estates or golf courses, and that many farmers have found it necessary to tear up old hedges and ditches where they used to grow so happily. Given a degree of moisture, so that they don't dry out in hot summers, one plant will soon generate a lot of youngsters in the garden and provide ample flowers to make up posies for the house.

Most of the narcissus family that I grow in this garden are cream or white varieties and are later flowering than many of the yellow strains. But I have a lot of the miniature yellow ones which are among the first to flower, notably the Cyclamineus cultivars 'Jumblie' and 'Tête-à-tête'. They're wonderful for small flower arrangements, flowering for weeks in the garden, and furthermore increase rapidly, providing a long-term source of colour both there and in the house. A great favourite of mine for flower-arranging in mid-spring is the daffodil 'Mrs R. O. Backhouse', a large-cupped cultivar. It has a very refined flower of almost unique colouring. The ivory-white perianth sets off the long, creamy shell-pink, trumpet crown, and the colour improves as it ages and fades gently. It lasts well in water and is delightful. Purists may well be horrified at the thought of a pink daffodil, but it is very subtle, starting off as a creamy-apricot before fading to a pink tinge which blends well with the milk-white perianth. It is beautiful as a cut flower for the house, very free flowering and a rapid increaser in the garden. The Poeticus cultivar 'Actaea' looks exquisite arranged with young spring foliage and blossom. It has a pure white perianth and a startling, tiny, red pheasant-eye centre, which makes a lovely fresh crisp display. It is almost identical to the species Poeticus 'pheasant eye' narcissus (*N. poeticus*), except that it is a little larger, flowers earlier and is easier to establish. They are both sweetly scented and among my favourites. It is a great joy to have enough daffodils to pick in armfuls without creating gaps in the garden and to provide huge vases of flowers around the house again early in the year. They are all beautiful cut flowers whether arranged carefully or bunched in a vase on their own, and their delicate spring perfume can be appreciated more fully indoors.

The first of the tulips overlap the daffodils and they are also good for picking as they never need to be arranged. They do that for themselves, stretching and waving their long stalks into lovely shapes and opening wide their faces in the warmth of the central heating. Among the first of the tulips here is 'Purissima' ('White Emperor'). It has huge primrose goblets which fade gently to milky white. Another lovely one is the single, late, cottage tulip 'Rosy Wings', which I have planted along the edge of the path under the pergola and which I am able to cut for the house in late spring. It is particularly good for picking, with long flowers of a very distinctive shape. Tulips are very economical for flower arranging as you only need half a dozen or so to make a lovely display. With the wide range available they can be

The ethereal, lime-green sprays of Alchemilla mollis, *here by the pond, associate well with foliage plants and are a 'must' for flower arranging.*

enjoyed both in the garden and the house during the spring and early summer months, and can suit any colour scheme. I was never tempted to grow them until we came here as I associated them with formal planting schemes in public parks and along seaside promenades, growing in serried rows and stiff military formation in the inevitable company of forget-me-nots and wallflowers. But planted in the garden in generous groups, they look very effective and provide a lovely show, filling the otherwise long gap between the last of the daffodils and early spring bulbs and the first of the roses and main herbaceous perennials. This garden would be very much poorer without them.

Once into early summer the riches produced in the garden for enjoyment in the house increase daily. Lovely blue or white *Campanula persicifolia* has already made its presence known, and if you've been lucky with its seedlings it will have popped up in all sorts of places where they won't be missed when picked. It will keep fresh and pretty in water for weeks on end with a seemingly never-ending succession of buds coming into bloom. One of my favourite and easiest flower arrangements in early summer is to put these campanulas with *Alchemilla mollis*, sometimes with an addition of blue or white polemonium. I could never say too much about the virtues of alchemilla as a cut flower. It is every flower arranger's dream, having sprays of tiny lime-green flowers on long wiry stems which are exquisite on their own or will enhance any arrangement or colour scheme. For use in the house I could never have too much of it in the garden,

ABOVE LEFT *The thistle-like flowers of* Eryngium variifolium *contrast well with the generous rounded blooms of* Paeonia lactiflora *'Bowl of Beauty'.*

LEFT *Blue polemonium, Jacob's ladder, make an ideal accompaniment to many other flowers for arrangements in the house.*

where its value is of equal importance. Somebody once said to me that you can never be too rich, too thin, or have too much alchemilla! There's not much chance of having too little as it seeds more freely than any other plant that I know, but it can be forgiven this rather wicked habit because of its sheer loveliness and its value as a cut flower.

Hosta leaves, ferns and grasses are all standing by as accompaniments to roses, irises, paeonies and the first delphiniums, as well as a wide range of blossom and flowering shrubs. Blue or purple *Iris sibirica* and the snowball flowers of *Virburnum opulus sterile* make a lovely combination. 'Iceberg' roses look and smell wonderful in a vase on their own with their prolific flowers and exquisite scent or with almost any foliage from the garden. It is such a generous rose giving of its best for so long throughout the summer and autumn, often with one or two blooms still hanging on at Christmas, and it is a delight as a cut flower. In early summer many of the old-fashioned shrub roses are coming into their own. My first introduction to these was shortly after I was married and had a neighbour whose garden was filled with them. She used to cut large bunches and leave them for me on the wall between our two gardens and never having encountered them before I could hardly believe that anything could be so beautiful. That was the start of my love affair with them, but it was to be many years before I would have a suitable garden where I could grow them and indulge my passion. Other floribunda and hybrid tea roses also make very good cut-flowers as do many of the ramblers and climbers. A simple bowl of the shell-pink blooms of climber 'New Dawn' makes a lovely centre-piece on a well-polished dining table.

I have a small patch of garden which is very arid and starved, being close to the ash tree in the hedge at the entrance to the garden. Here I abandon plants which are too invasive and exuberant to risk in the already overcrowded borders but which I would be sad to be totally deprived of. Some of them make wonderful cut flowers including *Achillea ptarmica* 'The Pearl', a white sidalcea and a tiny-flowered, airy white aster. All three of these would devour a complete border by mid-summer if well fed and watered, but by depriving them of a rich diet I'm able to contain them. They can't do any real harm where they are and where they have to compete with other potential thugs, like the carpeting *Symphytum* 'Roseum' and *Geranium procurrens*, and with *Brunnera macrophylla*, which has sprays of stunning, brilliant-blue flowers in the spring but great mounds of large, leathery, heart-shaped leaves that hang on throughout the summer. The brunnera seeds liberally, putting down deep roots which are not easily pulled out. If you miss the seedlings then you actually have to dig them out which can disturb their neighbours. These are all ideal in a woodland or semi-wild setting and at the same time provide me with a good source of flower-arranging material. Foxgloves and cow parsley also give a wonderful display in the house, and they too don't need arranging, looking perfectly lovely as they are, placed in a tall vase or jug.

ABOVE *Sweetly scented 'Iceberg' roses perfume the house, here arranged in a vase with slate blue hosta leaves.*

RIGHT *Hydrangeas, roses, schizostylis, allium seedheads and* Rosa glauca *hips provide interesting late-summer fruit and flowers for arrangements.*

A shrub which can hold its own alone in a vase is *Stephanandra incisa*, particularly in spring when the fresh young leaves are unfurling on rich-reddish-brown stems. Its arching habit makes it ideal for a large simple arrangement, and it is also a most attractive garden shrub all the year round, including the winter months when the coloured bark provides interest. Another useful shrub for flower arrangements is *Physocarpus opulifolius* 'Dart's Gold', which makes a lovely accompaniment to daffodils and tulips. The young butter-yellow foliage is joined by small clusters of tiny white flowers in late spring, giving a very dainty effect in any spring arrangement.

I like to use alliums in flower arrangements, because they last for weeks in water and their interesting shapes associate well with other flowers and foliage. Spiky iris leaves and the rounded and heart-shaped leaves of some hostas give a geometric quality when used with the globular heads of some of the larger alliums. Ferns and grasses look good mixed with the more pendulous types, as do other mixed flowers. Allium seed heads, too, provide interesting shapes in flower arrangements.

All forms of daisies enhance floral displays with their simple structured flowers and clear colours. A friend of ours always used to grow cornflowers in order to have a vase of them in her house and arranged them with white shasta daisies, creating a stunning effect. To achieve a simple, natural effect a few ears of ripe corn could be added and the shasta daisies replaced by the wild marguerites that adorn banks along many roads. I grow some on a bank where cowslips, primroses and wild daffodils proliferate in the spring.

My autumn garden is not yet complete as I haven't any dahlias or chrysanthemums, both of which make very good cut flowers for the house, but I grow several varieties of *Schizostylis coccinea* (Kaffir lily), which are perfect for cutting in the autumn with their pink, white or red flowers. There have even been occasions when I have been able to add schizostylis to Christmas flower arrangements, the coral-red variety being particularly appropriate in the festive season. Even in the depths of winter, there's always a twig, a spray of evergreen leaves, a sprig of rose hips, or even a lichen-covered branch that can be used to good effect in the house, perhaps with a few bought fresh flowers, dried ones, or even some of the lovely silk ones, of which there is such an enormous choice in the shops.

Arranging flowers and foliage, shapes and colours can also help on a small scale with planning planting schemes in the garden. By using different combinations in a vase I can often get ideas as to how to apply the same association to a flower bed. I had always promised myself that whenever I had a large enough garden I would grow enough flowers to enable me to pick sufficient for the house without leaving bare patches outside, and this has been one of my great joys here. Also it is always nice to be able to give some to friends who may not be fortunate enough to have a garden. Of course when the weather is good I prefer to enjoy the flowers in the garden, rather than bringing them into the house, but in bad weather I never hesitate to pick as many as possible. If I can't enjoy them outside I like to bring some of them indoors rather than leaving them to get battered by wind and rain.

Where once we had a productive vegetable garden, there is now a nursery with rows of plants in pots, which await visitors to take them to new homes and also provide a source of potted plants for the house.

FIRM FRIENDS
— AND —
FAVOURITES

I'M OFTEN ASKED about my favourite flower or plant, but I find it impossible to name just one, for there are so many with their own individual qualities to recommend them. Also with plants, as with everything else, my tastes change over the years, but there are many that have stood the test of time in my affections and that, no matter how small a garden I may have, I would never wish to be without. In endeavouring to enumerate my current favourites I am going to cheat a little, choosing families in many cases but singling out some members which are special friends. If I were to list favourites for each season, the task would be a little simpler as I would choose them for their performance and value at a particular time of year. For example, much as I love spring bulbs, I don't necessarily long to have daffodils and tulips popping up in summer and autumn. Equally, I prefer the warm colours and frosty smell of chrysanthemums at Christmas rather than roses, but find it very difficult to be appreciative or enthusiastic if I'm given them at Easter or in the spring. Once Christmastime is over I instinctively like to have daffodils, hyacinths and violets scenting the house. By the same token strawberries always taste better on a warm summer's day than on a cold frosty winter's one. My list of favourite plants grows continually as I make the acquaintance of more and more varieties.

FLOWERS

There are many ingredients that can be used in the making of a pretty garden: trees, shrubs, lawns, paths, water and foliage, but when we think of gardens most of us immediately think of flowers, especially of herbaceous plants and bulbs. They provide constant new interest and a wide diversity of colour, stature and perfume throughout the year. They are frequently the main stars but also serve to garnish, decorate and provide the filling in all areas of a garden. A garden without flowers is never really complete – like a house devoid of soft furnishings and ornaments – so their role is one of the most significant in the overall, all-year-round impact that a garden makes on the eye.

Roses

I can't believe there is anyone who doesn't like roses in one form or another, so they really must top my list, not least because they are synonymous with an English cottage garden. I have an unashamed passion for the old-fashioned shrub roses with their enormously generous dollops of bloom, wonderful colours ranging from purest white to rich, dark, grape-purple, and their heady perfumes. Not all of

Rosa 'Madame Isaac Pereire' produces enormous, richly scented blooms in abundance throughout the summer months.

The simplicity of the dog rose-like flower of Rosa glauca _is shown to best advantage against its own, striking, dusky-mauve foliage and purple stems._

them are scented but they manage to make up for this lack in other ways. People often complain that some only flower once in a season, but then so do many other plants, and many of them certainly for not as long as the shrub roses which bloom for anything up to six weeks or more. Quite a number of them are repeat flowering and others provide autumn colouring with a wonderful display of jewelled hips. The other criticism of course is that you do need quite a large space for most of them. Many a time I have chosen from a catalogue a rose which has been described as ideal for a small garden, but which has grown to be absolutely enormous, smothering everything in its wake and proving to be far from suitable for a limited space. However,

contrary to what the books may say about there being no need to prune them, I have found that you can and I do – hard! I usually set about them just after they have finished flowering, reducing them to rather sad-looking creatures, but it isn't long before they burst into life again putting on fresh young vigorous growth and foliage.

If I could only have one rose in the garden I think it would have to be _Rose rubrifolia_, or _Rosa glauca_ as it is now called – not nearly such an attractive name. (Why is it necessary to keep changing the names of plants? As fast as I manage to get my tongue round some almost unpronounceable name it is changed, and I have to start all over again!) _R. rubrifolia_, alias _R. glauca_, has the most wonderful purple stems and bluish grey foliage. Once it reaches a reasonable size – usually after only a couple of years from a seedling – it starts producing dainty, pink, dogrose flowers, so effective against the dusky leaves. These are followed by a generous crop of scarlet hips, often before the plant has defoliated, which linger on right through the winter, providing a feast for the birds who scatter the seeds around the garden with the result that seedlings crop up everwhere the following spring. Under one particularly vigorous _R. glauca_ shrub I'm rewarded with a complete carpet of seedlings every year, which I pot up and grow on.

For sheer long-term value from foliage, flowers, hips and rapid growth, this rose is unbeatable. It can be grown as a standard tree or pruned into any shape you want, keeping it small and compact or allowing it, as I do, to grow into a huge arching shrub. It is totally unfussy, will grow anywhere and is virtually disease free. You really can't ask much more of any plant. It does always have the last word, though: just when you think you have got it into shape, almost

The simple flowers of Rosa glauca _are replaced by clusters of scarlet hips, which ripen long before the leaves have fallen and linger on through the winter months._

overnight its hips swell, and particularly if it has the help of some rain, it suddenly goes into a deep curtsy, providing a crinoline over everything and anything nearby. There are several places in this garden where by late summer you have almost to go on hands and knees in order to get through to the adjoining area. It's almost as if the rose is saying to you after flowering: 'So you think my performance is over, but just wait for my star turn!' Before you realize it, the hips are ripe and begin to glow like jewels all over the garden, as if the Christmas lights had been turned on a little early. It is one of the first reminders that autumn is just round the corner. I grow *R. glauca* all over the garden, mainly at the back of borders where I prune them from below to maximize the space and allow me to underplant

them, usually with shade-tolerant plants, but also because I prefer large, arching shrubs like these to have their natural, flowing movement rather than stunted, contorted, tortured shapes.

Hellebores

As autumn arrives and dull winter days loom ever nearer, plants like cyclamen and *saxifraga fortunei* cheer me up, providing a sparkle of colour in the garden and filling me with a vain hope that summer isn't quite over, but when those dreary, cold, winter and early-spring days are upon us, there are plants which, by performing very early in the year, brighten up the winter garden. Among them are of course the glorious selections of hellebores, some of which even

The freckles and blushes of many Helleborus orientalis *can often only be appreciated by getting down on hands and knees.*

Helleborus corsicus *is one of the loveliest green-flowered plants, with glossy, prickly edged leaves and soft, velvety petals.*

start flowering in late autumn. Although winter- and spring-flowering, they perform well throughout the year with their lovely glossy foliage.

In mid-winter, when I have just about given up all hope of ever seeing any sign of life in the garden again, *Helleborus orientalis* begins to stir from its winter sleep and to thrust its thick bud-ladened stalks through the cold, barren ground. Soon the buds start to open into lovely cup-shaped flowers in shades of green, pink, purple and white. Admittedly you have to get down on your hands and knees to appreciate their full beauty as they hang down, demurely hiding their blushes and freckles on the inside of their petals. They bloom over a long period, and even after the flowers have died, they still hang there like faded silk petticoats. I prefer to leave them on as long as possible, certainly until the seeds have ripened and scattered – this is usually about mid-summer – so that the following spring I am rewarded with lots of seedlings. It can be very exciting if you have different colours of *H. orientalis* in the garden; the bees cross-pollinate them and you never know what colours you will get until the seedlings reach flowering-size two or three years later.

H. corsicus (*H. argutifolius*) is another great favourite of mine. When well grown it is a dramatic plant with glistening foliage supported on strong stalks, and enormous clusters of large cup-shaped apple-green flowers which seemingly last forever. Lime- and apple-green flowers are among my favourites and are a wonderful foil for other colours.

Around mid-winter it is worthwhile cutting off all the old foliage of *H. orientalis*. It leaves rather a gap for a short while in an already rather bare winter landscape but enables you to appreciate the flowering shoots as they emerge and shows them off to best advantage. The plant soon starts producing fresh young growth. With *H. argutifolius* I generally remove the old tatty leaves after flowering, once the young new foliage has started to appear. Both provide good architectural and textural shapes until the following winter, but the greatest joy is that they are so welcome and such a beautiful gift at a dreary time of year. Each winter I wish I had more of them in the garden and promise myself to rectify the situation. I know of one private garden where whole areas are carpeted with *H. orientalis* in full bloom from mid-winter to early spring, and you could be forgiven for forgetting that you are in a winter garden, as there is so much colour and foliage, particularly when the snowdrops arrive to keep the hellebores company. There has been an enormous revival of interest in this lovely family of plants in recent years, enriching both gardeners and their gardens.

Alliums

It would be a bit of a cheat to lump all bulbs together, so I've decided just to mention a few favourite alliums. These are plants that I have come to appreciate relatively recently. Not only are they easy to accommodate in a densely planted garden but they seem to benefit from it, because their onion-flower heads, which are often almost too heavy for their wiry stalks, get much-needed support from surrounding plants. The wide variety available provides long-term cover.

Of the ones I grow, the first to bloom is *Allium aflatunense*, which has large, deep-lilac flower heads in late spring, following on from the early-flowering tulips and associating well with the later varieties. A very pretty, pale shell-pink allium follows, standing about 12 to 15 inches (30–38cm) tall. It arrived uninvited from somewhere and seeds itself about. I suspect I shall have to keep an eye on this one as it could become a little too enthusiastic and

The dainty chandelier bells of Allium cernuum *are best appreciated on a raised wall, in a rock garden or at the front of a sunny border.*

crop up everywhere. *A. albopilosum* (*A. christophii*) never fails to charm and surprise, and cause comment with its enormous heads of shimmering silver-lilac stars on short stalks, which still look stunning long after the flowers have faded. Another favourite is the pingpong-ball-sized, aptly named *A. azureum* (*A. caeruleum*). This is a truly lovely sky-blue colour and lingers on in flower for several weeks through early summer. It stands about 18 inches (45 cm) high and looks wonderful with acid-green euphorbias, magenta geraniums and many other accompaniments.

Then the lilac and purple shades return, first of all with the little chandelier bells of *A. cernuum*, followed in mid-summer and on into late summer by *A. pulchellum* (*A. carinatum, A. cirrhosum*) with its bewhiskered wheat-eared blooms hanging down in tassels in great profusion. It breeds prodigiously and can be

a bit of a nuisance but is so lovely and is such a wonderful cut flower for arranging in the house that it can be forgiven. To avoid a total invasion you can always cut it back before it seeds, but the temptation is to leave the dead heads in place, as they, too, are decorative. I have recently acquired a few precious bulbs of a white form, which is exquisite, and I'm hoping that in time it will increase as generously.

In hot pursuit comes the dramatic, dark grape-purple *A. sphaerocephalon*, known as the drumstick allium, although the heads are shaped more like a large chicken's egg, standing proud on 3-foot (1m)-high stems. They are great fun and a really good architectural addition to the summer border. Earlier on, the tiny *A. ostrowskianum* (*A. oreophilum*), with lilac-pink bells, flowers on a small rock wall, and last of all to bloom here is another tiny variety, *A. kansuense* (*A. sikkimense*, *A. tibeticum*). Standing erect on wiry stalks about 6 inches (15 cm) high, with fine foliage, it produces little nodding heads of almost navy blue – a real charmer.

There are of course many more varieties but so far these are the ones that I grow here. They are a wonderful family; I find them easy, generous (as they seed and increase liberally), long lasting and ideal for flower arranging, used either as fresh flowers or as seed heads in dried-flower arrangements.

Campanulas

We would certainly be a lot poorer without campanulas in our gardens. What a lovely family they are – from the tiny members with starry flowers to the large blowzy Canterbury bells – and such a large family that I'm only going to touch on a few which are old and trusted friends of mine. Among

Campanula persicifolia *flowers for months throughout the summer if regularly deadheaded.*

Campanula latifolia *bells vary in shades from pure white to purple. Here lilac-tinged buds open out into silvery flowers.*

have to leave some seed heads on at the end of the season in order to get the seedlings but it can also be propagated very easily by division at any time. Apart from the obvious charm of its colour and form, and general usefulness in the garden, it makes the most wonderful cut flower for the house, where again, if you remove the dead heads, it will keep fresh and pretty in water for weeks on end with a seemingly never-ending succession of buds coming into bloom.

Among the tall campanulas is C. *latifolia*, which is a lovely, stately plant producing long tubular bells in varying shades of violet, purple and palest lilac, but probably the most eye-catching is C. *l. alba*, whose bellflowers are the purest, virginal white. It does need some support being so tall and carrying such an abundance of flowers, but in a more sheltered position than I am able to provide in my windy garden it would probably fare better under its own steam.

C. *trachelium* 'Alba Flore Pleno' never fails to cause comment when it is in bloom, with its white, frilly-knickerbocker bells in generous abundance for weeks on end. Standing about 24 inches (60 cm) high, it can be given pride of place in the front of the border, where it can be shown off to best advantage. It doesn't like wet weather, which turns the delicate blooms soggy and brown and very dejected-looking, and it may need a little cosseting at first, but that is no more than it deserves, and given time it will more than repay your patience. I have recently acquired C. *t.* 'Bernice' which shows all the promise of being another lovely addition with double violet-blue flowers, which associate well with the old roses and geraniums in the garden. On the whole I prefer single flowers to double ones, but these two campanulas with their frilly petals are especially dainty and charming and not in the least blowzy.

Of the smaller varieties C. *carpatica* 'White Clips' is a delight. On a rockery or a wall it makes a pretty

those at the top of my list of favourites has to be *Campanula persicifolia*. Emerging from rosettes of glossy leaves on erect wiry stems, enlarged harebell flowers in shades of blue or white are produced continually for two months or more, provided you keep nipping off the dead flowers. It seems happy anywhere and seeds prolifically all over the garden, be it on dry banks, in shady areas, or amongst all the herbaceous plants and the shrubs. Obviously you cushion of upturned, pure-white chalices. It is another plant that seemingly flowers forever if you can find the time and patience to nip off dead heads. There are various blue forms as well. A pretty and easy small form is *C. cochleariifolia*, the fairy's thimble, which makes tufted growth as it spreads horizontally with harebell flowers in blue or white on long wiry stems all summer. It looks just like a prostrate form of the lovely wild harebell which mingles with the wild thyme and scabious on the downs. *C. sarmatica* is a lovely variety for a sunny position in the front of a border. It has soft, hairy, green leaves above which rise the stems carrying downy, grey-blue flowers. It's a beautiful, unusual and showy plant. As yet mine is still fairly small and I'm looking forward to it growing up.

The lovely, soft-dusky-pink *C. lactiflora* 'Loddon Anna' is exquisite in colour but standing at over 6 feet (2 m) is really not at its best here in my windswept garden. But I have heard that, if you cut it back before it reaches its full size, it will not inhibit flowering but will help keep the whole plant to more manageable and wind-tolerant proportions. At the other end of the scale *C. l.* 'Pouffe' grows to only about 12 to 18 inches (30–45 cm) and makes a pretty mound for the front of the border, but it too benefits from a little propping up on crutches. Another favourite campanula is *C. latiloba*, a good weed-suppressing ground-cover plant, from which grow stiff erect spikes clothed with upward-facing rich-blue, lilac or white, cup-shaped flowers. It can be somewhat invasive, so you have to take care where you place it, but it is nonetheless a pretty and useful plant.

These are just a few members of this large and lovely family. There are many more to suit every-one's tastes and requirements, including some little gems for alpine and sink-garden enthusiasts, with flowers ranging from tiny thimbles to small bells.

Anemones

Several of the plant families I have chosen are favourites because I can have one or other member of the family in flower for most of the year. The anemones certainly come into this category as some are among the first and the last flowers to bloom. The first to appear here is the little *Anemone blanda* in all its pink, blue and white forms. When I have almost forgotten their existence, suddenly a tiny splash of blue – the first colour to make its appearance – emerges quite unexpectedly and unannounced in a bare patch of earth, unfurling shaggy petals from a ruff of leaves; like the miniature cyclamen, the flowers announce their arrival on the scene before the leaves. They open their little faces to weak late-winter and early-spring sunshine and seem to gather strength and courage from it as the

Anemone blanda are the first of the anemone family to bloom in my garden, and their little faces upturned to the sun are a welcome sight early in the year.

Pulsatilla vulgaris give long term interest in the garden, with soft ferny foliage and enchanting anemone flowers which are succeeded by tasselled seed heads.

weeks progress into spring. Here, if left well alone they increase generously, although the frost does tend to throw up the little tubers, which then need to be tucked back into the ground.

In a wild area I also grow the little wood amenone, *A. nemorosa*. Once established it runs about and naturalizes rapidly, so is ideal for woodland or wild areas of the garden, and for me its charm and nostalgic quality (reminding me of childhood walks) make it worth finding a home for. It grows here on 'the great wall of China' behind the patio, in the company of *A. blanda*, primroses and violets. The anemone-like *Pulsatilla vulgaris*, known as the Pasque flower, starts to bloom around Easter and is such a pretty thing and full of surprises. It merits a place for its soft fern-like foliage alone, but its rich, velvety, anemone-like blooms in deep purples, reds, pinks and whites are some of the stars of the spring garden. But its performance doesn't end there, as its flowers

are followed by fluffy, tassel seed heads which adorn the plant well into summer.

In early spring a few of the lovely *A. pavonina*, in shades ranging from bright red to salmon pink, come up in the grass under the medlar tree, but it really is time I moved them, because, apart from competing with the tree and the grass for both light and food, they are also prey to Len and the lawnmower. Some more little nomads which must be moved on for their own good. Poor Len, there are so many precious treasures in unexpected places that he hardly dare set his feet down anywhere and isn't even safe on the lawns.

One of the stars of my borders is the very beautiful *A. rivularis* which flowers in early summer. It has stiff branching stems carrying a long succession of pure-white flowers with amazing metallic gunmetal-blue reverses and blue anthers, followed by attractive Sputnik-shaped seed pods. I leave these on to ripen, to allow it to self-seed, or to collect for propagation to grow the following year. It is a truly lovely plant and one whose acquaintance I have only recently made.

Then from mid-summer onwards we start to enjoy the Japanese anemone hybrids. They are the stars in my late-summer and autumn garden and have a flowering period of anything up to three months. I grow different varieties here ranging from pure white and pale pink to semi-double pink and deep pink. I have given up trying to name them all, as there are such subtle differences between so many of them that without an expert I would certainly get it wrong. *A.* × *hybrida* 'Honorine Jobert' (*A. japonica* 'Honorine Jobert') is considered the best white form and certainly gives a wonderful display. *A.* × *h* 'Superba' (*A. j.* Superba') has silver-pink flowers and

Japanese anemone hybrids are the mainstay of the late summer garden. Tall stately plants that require little or no staking, they sometimes flower for up to three months.

Lilium regale is one of the easiest and loveliest lilies to grow and has an almost intoxicating perfume.

starts blooming as early as mid-summer, thus extending the season even longer with many of the others flowering late into autumn. They take some time – anything up to a couple of years – to settle down and get established, but once they do, they romp away and you may have to be fairly ruthless thinning them out. In dry conditions they are likely to be a bit more hesitant. I'm trying to establish them along the borders of the path under the pergola to provide late-summer interest after the delphiniums and shrub roses have been cut back, but just where I'm prepared to give them their head, they are proving very shy. They do look charming bordering the paths, and it's a joy to have their soft pastel shades at a time of year when there are so many hot colours about.

I couldn't say that any one anemone is a favourite as I'm very fond of them all – each being so lovely in its own season – but, since I have only recently discovered *A. rivularis*, that for the time being has found a big place in my affections.

Lilies

I've mentioned lilies elsewhere, mainly in relation to their perfume, and although many don't have a scent, their sheer beauty of shape and their colour range still make them great favourites of mine. Like alliums they are easy to accommodate, as they can be planted in and amongst herbaceous plants and shrubs, so that they come up between them and benefit from the support of their neighbours. Of all the exotic-looking and exquisite varieties available, *Lilium regale* is still one of the loveliest. It is probably one of the easiest to grow, and unlike many others is lime-tolerant. Once it is settled in a particular position it will increase generously and reward you with a lovely display of its huge trumpet blooms in mid-summer, filling the garden with its heady perfume, particularly on warm, balmy, summer evenings.

I've found that martagon lilies are funny things. They have never yet appeared for me the year following planting and as a result have often been damaged or dug up, when I have forgotten the bulbs were there. If they do escape that fate, they then put in an appearance the following year. After planting their bulbs for several years I am at last beginning to have a reasonable show of *L. martagon*, and I believe that once they are established they readily increase to provide a good display. They are very charming with purple or white Turkscap flowers and will grow and naturalize in grass and under trees, which can be so useful.

L. pardalinum is a variety that is not shy to breed, and will perform well in dry spots. I have now abandoned mine to possibly the driest and most arid position in the garden, under the plum trees. Originally I planted only a half dozen or so bulbs in a relatively moist, sunny spot, where they rapidly took over and swamped everything in their wake. Beautiful and spectacular as they are with stems over 6 feet (2 m) high and yellow-spotted, orange Turkscap flowers, they were just too enthusiastic, and I had to dig them up. My original half-dozen bulbs generated two sackfuls, and I still find the odd 'one that got away'.

For two years now I have grown *L. tigrinum* 'Pink Beauty' in a large earthenware pot. This really is a beauty. It has soft dusky coral-pink flowers on tall dark stems and is clothed in dark leaves – a

wonderful contrast between stems, foliage and flowers. They bloom for weeks on end, still managing to look stately and lovely even when down to the last few remaining buds at the tip of their stalks. The youngsters have sported one single flower – not bad for a mere one-year-old – so now it is time for them to be separated from mother and sent out into the world under their own steam, to be potted up or planted out individually.

The dramatic, orange, turkscap flowers of Lilium pardalinum *with their pollen-laden anthers are produced on stems reaching up to 7 feet (2.2m).*

I'm still struggling to get a good clump of the Madonna lily, *L. candicans*. I believe they require some lime, and having a neutral-to-acid soil here, this could be the reason they don't do very well for me. However, the ones that are here haven't died yet, so I'm hopeful that one day, with time and patience, I may have a good display of them. They really are worth the effort, although I sometimes wonder if it isn't neglect that they prefer, for I have often seen them flourishing in huge clumps in corners of totally overgrown, little cottage gardens.

The bulb catalogues list numerous varieties of lilies with mouth-watering descriptions, often with illustrations, so you can make your own selection according to personal taste and to suit any colour scheme in the garden, or simply for pot culture. However they do appreciate a little love with regular feeding in the growing season, and if you ensure they don't dry out after blooming they will reward you with their spectacular and often exotic flowers. I believe no summer garden should be without lilies. They take up little space, and there are so many different varieties that you can have one or other flowering from early summer through to early autumn. But don't plant them singly – they look so lonely. Three, five or more make a good clump and a pleasing impact.

The hot electric colour of Phlox paniculata *'Starfire' glows in a late summer border.*

Phlox

Some people don't grow phlox as they dislike the smell, but I find that it is very much a part of their appeal. I love the slightly old, musky, almost musty scent that wafts from them throughout the late-summer garden. It is a perfume evocative of long, hot, childhood summer days. Why is it, I wonder,

that we always remember our childhood summers as having endless sunshine, and our winters always with snow, tinkling icicles and snowmen? Many of the colours of the *Phlox paniculata* varieties are hot and steamy like the late-summer days when they bloom, but the wonderful spectrum of colour they offer ranges through pure, almost opalescent white, softest pinks, cool lilacs and mauves, coral, vibrant-hot, almost luminous reds and darkest purples. They provide richness and wealth to the late-summer border and associate so well with their bedfellows, which also revel in the same conditions. One of the borders to the rear of the cottage is ideal for them, having a good, deep, moisture-retentive soil, and it really comes into its own in late summer and early autumn. Here I grow a wide selection of phlox in the company of aconitums, echinaceas (cone flower),

The stately speciosum lilies with their spectacular blooms prolong the lily season for many weeks through early autumn and often into mid-autumn.

A wide colour range of **Phlox** paniculata *flowers is available, including many which have a contrasting eye.*

cimicifugas, physostegias (obedient plant), lythrums (purple loosestrife) and the ethereal wands of *Thalictrum dipterocarpum* bringing up the rear – all creating a rich tapestry of colour.

I don't know the names of all the *P. paniculata* that I grow as I have acquired them over the years from generous friends, but I do have the electric-red 'Starfire', pure-white 'White Admiral', dark-purple 'Border Gem', coral 'Brigadier', deep-pink, darker-eyed 'Sandringham', soft-pink 'Mother of Pearl' and creamy-pink 'Elizabeth Arden'. In addition to these there are others in different shades of lilac, pink and mauve, including some with contrasting eyes. One of my great favourites, however, is the species *P. paniculata* which has tall, willowy stems topped by large panicles of smaller but very refined lilac flowers. Very easy to grow, and quick to make a large clump, it generates an aura of quiet loveliness and cool elegance to offset some of the blowziness of some of its cousins.

Smaller but equally refined, and very rewarding in their long flowering season, are *P. maculata* 'Alpha', 'Omega' and 'Miss Lingard'. *P. m.* 'Alpha' has soft lilac-pink flowers, *P. m.* 'Omega' is white with a lilac eye and *P. m.* 'Miss Lingard' is pure white. The flowers clothe almost half the 3-foot (1m) stems in long, cylindrical heads and bloom for weeks on end. Secondary blooms are produced from the lower leaf-axils if you remove the top flowers as they fade, thus extending the flowering season. They are very elegant plants with attractive foliage to offset the lovely flowers. Being somewhat smaller than *P. paniculata*, they would probably be easier to accommodate in a small garden where their proportions would make a better balance. They all make good cut-flowers and continue flowering in water for some time if you don't mind picking up the discarded blooms on a daily basis. Their soft perfume hangs about the house like real pot-pourri, unlike the products sold in shops which are artificially scented and, I think, smell more like bathroom freshener than dried garden flowers.

Delphiniums

Delphiniums are such a familiar part of the English garden scene that there is little I can say except to extol their beauty. No other flower that I know offers such a range of wonderful shades of blue, mauve and purple. There are grey, yellow and even red varieties, though I don't have any longing for these any more than I wish that someone would breed a blue or purple daffodil. The grace, stature and colours of the good, old-fashioned garden types are more than enough for me, but I would find it difficult to choose one particular shade of colour that I have a preference for.

Delphiniums associate well with old roses and other cottage-garden plants.

Although delphiniums are easy enough to grow almost anywhere, there are one or two difficulties in their cultivation. The hardest to overcome is that of slugs and snails. If hostas are caviar to them, then delphiniums must be what any food is to a starving man, for they certainly demolish them with as much relish, more often than not before the young shoots have even emerged from the ground. All sorts of remedies are offered, including of course, the use of slug pellets, which are very effective if applied on a regular basis. Many people prefer not to use them for fear of harming other wildlife in the garden or domestic animals. Holly leaves, sharp grit and gravel, or anything rough or thorny are good deterrents, as slugs in particular don't like moving over abrasive materials which could damage them.

Another problem with delphiniums is how to show the plant off to its best advantage. Its stature, which is one of its attributes, can also bring about its downfall – literally. The exuberance and abundance of the flower spikes can be too much for the rather brittle, hollow stems to cope with, particularly in wet weather when the whole plant becomes top heavy with the added weight of the rain. To overcome this I have found that the best way to plant them is between shrubs and small trees, on which they can lean when the elements get the better of them. This also helps with the other difficulty of filling the not-inconsiderable gap delphiniums leave behind after flowering, when they have been cut back to the ground, as the shrubs and trees will help to hide the gap. However the delphiniums do soon generate new growth and usually produce a second flush of flowers in mid-autumn, not on quite such a grand scale as in the summer, but very welcome nonetheless. They provide a wonderful and theatrical display in the summer in the company of old roses and at a time when the majority of the herbaceous perennials are still waiting in the wings.

FOLIAGE AND FORM

Foliage plays an important role in the general overall appearance and shape of the garden, and many plants grown primarily for the colour or shape of their foliage also provide interest over a long period, often producing flowers as a bonus. In this category I'm going to lump together a number of plants not just for their architectural and textural value but also for their usefulness and benefit as companions to other plants, for their long-term interest and often for growing in shady, hot, baked, or simply awkward areas of the garden.

Hostas

The most popular and best known of all the foliage plants is probably the hosta family with its wide variety of leaf shape and colour. They are very good ground-cover plants as well as providing good architectural shapes. One of the reasons I find them so useful is that they can be interplanted with spring bulbs. These always present a problem with their tatty leaves which must be left hanging on for weeks after they have flowered. As the new hosta leaves unfurl they cover the dying leaves, allowing them to rot down in peace and unnoticed. With their variety of leaves, from narrow lance shapes to huge 'elephant ears', hostas associate well with other architectural plants like ferns, irises and alchemilla. Of course they are caviar to slugs and snails which are quite a problem to keep at bay and can produce something looking more like a Swiss-cheese plant than a hosta.

Foliage, with its wide range of shape, texture and colour, has a useful and important role to play in the garden.

I have quite a number of hostas in the garden, but if I had to choose one particular favourite I think *Hosta sieboldiana* var. *elegans* could well win the prize, with its massive blue-grey ridged leaves which turn butter-yellow in the autumn, and its white or pale-lilac flowers. It doesn't seem to be quite so delectable to snails as they don't attack it with quite the same vigour as they do some of the other varieties, particularly *H. fortunei* var. *albopicta*, which gets shredded out of existence the moment your back is turned. Although they are always recommended for damp shade, hostas are really very accommodating and grow almost anywhere. It's simply that they give their best performance when provided with some moisture and shade.

Euphorbias

Euphorbias are fast becoming some of my favourite plants. Here again it is possible to have different varieties, if not actually starring, certainly providing some interest throughout the entire year. Many of them are evergreen and provide shape and form in the winter months, producing their often spectacular flower heads later on. The most obvious of these is *Euphorbia characias* ssp. *wulfenii* with its tall, stately stems clothed in lance-shaped leaves and followed by enormous green and yellow heads in spring, which linger on for months. Another wonderful variety for winter interest is the slightly more tender *E. mellifera* whose foliage is wonderful all the year round. Given a sheltered corner from cold winter winds it soon grows into a spectacular specimen of shrub proportions.

As my gardening tastes change and mature, I find myself recognizing more and more the value of form and texture, and I also have a great weakness for lime- and acid-green flowers, which are the feature of so many members of the euphorbia family. As I discover more varieties, I find myself discarding other plants in favour of them. Many of them revel in dry conditions, so both benefit from and give of their best in hot dry summers which seem to be becoming more and more a feature of the English climate. In this garden the euphorbia season starts with *E. characias* ssp. *wulfenii* and *E. mellifera*, followed soon after by *E. polychroma* (*E. epithymoides*), the invasive *E. cyparissias*, and in turn the blue-grey leaves of *E. rigida* (*E. biglandulosa*), *E. nicaeensis* and *E. myrsinites*. These last three are all fairly prostrate and require a dry and well-drained, sunny position – ideal for banks, walls and patios. They are among the loveliest euphorbias with the contrast of the lime-green heads and blue foliage. As a bonus *E. nicaeensis* has bright pink stems to enhance it even more.

Another variety which is a great favourite of mine is *E. seguieriana* ssp. *niciciana*, which has wiry pink stems clothed in fine, needle, blue-green foliage and topped by small-flowered, acid-yellow heads, and what a performance and value it gives: flowering from late-spring through to mid-autumn – a real delight in the front of a sunny border. By chance, I planted *Allium azureum* in amongst it, where its true-blue flower heads look wonderful with the acid colouring of the euphorbia and with the blue *Baptisia australis* (false indigo) and a magenta-coloured tradescantia forming a backcloth. Yet another pink-stemmed variety is the tall late-summer-flowering *E. sikkimensis*. It prefers a bit more moisture than most of the euphorbia family but is rather like an unruly child and runs about energetically, so needs to be given space.

The wonderful architectural leaves of Hosta sieboldiana, *here accompanied by the tall spikes of* Iris orientalis, *rounded clumps of alchemilla, candelabra primulas and other hosta varieties around the pond.*

Much better behaved and certainly my current favourite is *E. schillingii* which is another mid- to late-summer-flowering variety. Tall erect stems, clothed in beautifully veined leaves and growing 4 to 5 feet (1.2-1.7 m) tall, are topped by saucer-sized flat heads of acid-green and yellow flowers. It looks superb with any of the late-summer herbaceous colour schemes – blue agapanthus, richly coloured phlox, hot-coloured crocosmia and dahlias, or any softer shades of pink, white and yellow. It associates well with everything, enhancing its neighbours and is a real jewel in the summer border. It is one of my great favourites not least because it was discovered in Nepal. Len spent many years serving in the

Brigade of Gurkhas, and we both have such fond memories of the delightful hill people of Nepal, who have served so loyally in the British army for well over a century. Now that Nepal has opened its doors in recent years to allow in tourists and visitors, a number of new and exciting plants are being introduced to the rest of the world. My hope is that its lovely people and the sheer beauty of the country will not be the poorer for this.

Another recent, exciting euphorbia introduction is *E. dulcis* 'Chameleon'. A seedling brought home from a hedgerow in the Dordogne in France by friends of ours was given to a nurseryman who successfully propagated it, winning an Award of

Euphorbia polychroma, one of the first euphorbias to flower, makes a dramatic impact in the spring with startling acid-yellow flower bracts over a long period.

Euphorbia schillingii *makes a wonderful contribution to the late summer border. Both flowers and foliage associate beautifully with any colour scheme.*

Euphorbia seguierana *spp.* niciciana *flowers from spring right through until autumn. Here it is growing with* Allium azureum.

Merit. They very generously gave me large clumps for my garden in the early days when it had only just become available and was a much sought-after plant, as indeed it still is. It has very dark, beetroot-maroon foliage and, grown as a large clump in full sun, it is very dramatic, though the leaves adopt a lighter metallic-green tone in shade. The flowers are insignificant and should be removed to encourage the young growth, which has the richest colouring and provides a good contrast to other perennials.

More familiar members of this fascinating family, such as *E. griffithii* 'Fireglow', *E. amygdaloides* 'Purpurea', *E. a.* var. *robbiae*, and others, are all readily available. I strongly recommend anyone who likes interesting foliage, and particularly if they have a hot, dry garden where it is difficult to grow things well, to have a closer look at euphorbias. You can't fail to find some that will be very garden-worthy and also give immense satisfaction and pleasure. Their sap can be caustic and may cause some irritation to the skin which is why some people won't grow them. However, if we knew and were concerned about the number of poisonous plants in our gardens, I think we might have very spotty, empty borders. I certainly would not want to be without foxglove (*Digitalis*) and monkshood (*Aconitum*) varieties, or laburnum and baneberry (*Actaea*), to name but a few poisonous but attractive garden plants. I wonder how many gardeners refuse to grow rhubarb because its leaves are poisonous. As a child I was not prepared to accept a warning of this without finding out for myself and was really quite poorly as a result. I suspect that a sampling of euphorbia leaves might have been more serious.

Ferns

Other groups of plants that are enjoying a revival of interest are the ferns. I know little about them as yet, except that I am just beginning to appreciate their true value. I don't know of any that have flowers, but there is a variety and perfection of foliage. I'm still experimenting with them as some can be a nuisance in a small garden, running about ad lib, but I keep adding to my small collection as I become more fascinated by them. Three particular varieties have become firm favourites. First the very lovely *Athyrium goeringianum* 'Pictum' (*A. niponicum metallicum*, *A. n. pictum*) known as the Japanese painted fern. The only possible disadvantage with this one is that it is not evergreen. I have to take care to mark its position, as it disappears in winter and when looking for new planting spaces in the spring I frequently damage some poor little thing still enjoying its winter sleep. When the young fronds emerge they unfurl on dark maroon stems and later open out with silver-grey glaucous leaves, which have a wonderful metallic sheen.

My other two favourites are varieties of *Polystichum setiferum*. Both are evergreen and are easy to grow almost anywhere. Their foliage remains lovely and fresh throughout the summer months in particular, and provides interest in the winter. I discovered by chance that their performance is enhanced if you cut out all the old fronds in the spring. One year the cats decided to use them as a trampoline, causing so much damage that the only solution was to cut the ferns right back to the base and then provide them with a wire-netting cage to protect them until they had re-grown. The result was stunning, as the young fronds emerged pristine and fresh without the distraction of the old, and by then rather tatty, foliage from the previous years. It was the old foliage, I think, that particularly attracted the cats, as the young foliage doesn't have the same amount of spring and is less appealing to them. Clumps of grasses are also prey to the same enthusiastic stamping and scratching.

Grasses

Grasses are very effective forms of foliage. I planted several different ones at the outset in this garden and have slowly been acquiring others as I have discovered them. Like the ferns, some of them run about recklessly, while others remain well behaved. Many cope with, and indeed thrive in, dry, starved conditions, while others prefer heavy damp soils. I started with *Stipa gigantea*, *Avena sempervirens* (*Helictotrichon sempervirens*) and *Festuca glauca*. All have stood the test of time in my affections and are still with us. *S. gigantea* makes a dense, low, weed-suppressing clump of narrow grey-green leaves, from which arise profuse, tall, flower stems that burst into huge heads of purple inflorescences. As they mature and open, they positively drip with little caterpillars of pollen. The whole effect in bloom is of a fountain, and quite lovely. Its beauty is shown off to best advantage when it it grown on a wall or any raised area. The flowers turn golden-yellow with age and remain attractive through autumn and into winter. The non-spreading *A. sempervirens* also makes a clump; it is smaller than the stipa in every way, but with intense-blue, narrow foliage topped by slender, arching, flower stems. *F. glauca* is smaller still, making cushions of needle-fine, steel-blue, tufted foliage with purple inflorescences. Both this and the

Polystichum setiferum *contrast well with rounded hostas, succulent* Sedum rosea, *variegated* Houttuynia cordata *'Chameleon' and spiky* Hakonechloa macra *'Aureola'.*

The lovely inflorescences of Stipa gigantea *resemble a fountain.*

they age. Planted in an east-west position where it will catch both the early-morning and late-evening sunshine, it takes on the appearance of tongues of ruby flames and the effect is startling and magical.

A grass that benefits from heavy, damp conditions is *Stipa arundinacea*, pheasant's tail grass. It has brownish-green evergreen leaves arching to about 18 inches (45 cm), and from them, in autumn, emerge needle-fine stems up to 3 feet (1m) or more, from which dangle dainty, pendant flower spikes. *Pennisetum alopecuroides*, another evergreen, is an autumn-flowering grass which produces black bottlebrushes. Its flat, grassy leaves make it ideal for the front of the border, provided some well-meaning friend doesn't mistake it for a clump of couch grass and pull it out. Its long flower spikes make it a good cut flower. A much larger plant is the one form of *Miscanthus* I have in the garden, probably *M. sinensis*. Although I've had to dispose of fairly large clumps due to lack of space, I like to keep one for the lovely musical sound it makes whenever the wind blows through it. It makes a wonderful wind filter and is a substitute for other plants like bamboo, which can also be planted as a screen to protect certain areas from wind damage. The stems remain upright and the dead leaves more or less intact for quite some time through the winter, continuing to provide shape and form and function as a wind filter.

avena revel in hot sunny positions on the front of a border or the edge of a path, where their lovely foliage produces its best colour and positively gleams in the sun. All three of these grasses are more or less evergreen, which is a great bonus in the winter.

Recently I've been thrilled and excited by a new purchase – *Imperata cylindrica* 'Rubra', Japanese blood grass. It has 12 to 18 inch (30–45 cm) blades which emerge emerald-green and turn dark-wine red as

Saxifrages

Another large family is that of the saxifrages and their related genera, which include heucheras and tiarellas, and among these I have some very definite favourites. No self-respecting cottage-style garden should be without at least one kind of the old-

Heuchera macrantha 'Palace Purple' *is both a useful and lovely foliage plant. The dainty flower spikes are a bonus and are shown off perfectly against the dark bronzed leaves.*

Tiarella cordifolia, aptly named the foam flower, only blooms in the spring, but the attractive, veined leaves on wiry runners give pretty ground cover throughout the year.

The tiny, starry flowers of the dainty Tiarella trifoliata *are produced from spring right through the summer. In a quiet way this is an exquisite little plant.*

fashioned London prides. The one I particularly like is a very dainty little one, *Saxifraga umbrosa* var. *primuloides*, which makes very flat, neat cushions of rosettes with the tiniest sprays of starry flowers on fine stalks not much more than 2 inches (5 cm) high. It spreads but is well-behaved and doesn't smother its neighbours in its enthusiasm. All the London prides make good weed-suppressing ground cover with pretty evergreen foliage.

A number of the heucheras and tiarellas are at least partially evergreen. One of the most popular is *Heuchera micrantha* 'Palace Purple' – not really purple at all but with good, dark, rich-maroon young foliage, which as it ages turns a metallic-bronze, retaining its beetroot colouring on the reverses and on the stalks. It doesn't like to be exposed to hot sun, which damages the leaves, but comes into its own in shade, particularly when in late summer it produces airy sprays of tiny pink-cream flowers on long wiry stems, a lovely contrast against the dark foliage.

My greatest favourites, however, are the *S. fortunei* varieties most especially *S. fortunei* 'Wada'. Its translucent red stalks are topped by rich, succulent, glossy, kidney-shaped leaves. As if this wonderful foliage wasn't reward enough from the moment it starts to appear in the spring, these saxifrages suddenly surprise you in autumn with huge panicles of starry, cream tassels. These rise above the rosettes of still-fresh leaves, lighting up a dull corner in the autumn garden, when so much is looking tired and getting ready to go to bed for the winter. A much smaller, earlier variety and also very charming is *S. cortusifolia fortunei* 'Rosea', with green leaves and dainty pink flowers. On a miniature scale is *S. fortunei* 'Mount Nachi', with dark, maroon leaves covered in tiny bristles which give them a spotted effect. This little plant is a real treasure.

At the other end of the year, in the spring, the tiarellas begin to perform. The first to flower here is *Tiarella cordifolia*, the foam flower. It makes lovely ground cover in a shady position, where it runs about on long, hairy stems covered in dainty light-green leaves with red-veined markings. In late spring and early summer these are topped by a cloud of foamy, starry, cream flowers, producing a lovely light effect under and amongst hellebores and with epimediums and erythroniums (dog's-tooth violets). *T. trifoliata* has even tinier flowers and continues from spring right through until late autumn. It doesn't run but makes generous clumps without too much effort. A group planting of this is sheer delight with its tiny little stars seemingly being produced forever, and is a real treasure for the fairies at the bottom of your garden! The queen of tiarellas is *T. wherryi*. The young foliage, stalks and flower buds are all a deep, crushed-raspberry pink, with flowers opening to become little, fluffy, pink candles being produced continually through the summer. Here again, a group planting is the most effective way of enjoying it to the full. All of these flourish in cool, woodland conditions requiring little or no sun to bloom generously, if provided with a nice humus-rich soil to encourage them.

ACKNOWLEDGEMENTS

I owe a debt of gratitude to the many people without whose support and encouragement this book would never have been written. My husband Len has been a tower of strength in the creation and maintenance of this garden. He has coped with being a gardening widower with endless patience and forbearance. Our daughter Antonia has ensured that we have not starved, and has patiently tried to explain the mysteries of a word processor to a mother who suffers from technophobia, frequently rescuing me from its terrors. I am especially grateful to Andrew Lawson for his wonderful photographs. His friendship and enthusiasm for my garden over the past three years have been invaluable.

I would also like to thank Michael Dover of Weidenfeld & Nicolson who gave me the opportunity and the confidence to write this book; and Colin Grant my editor who has patiently encouraged me and coaxed me to meet deadlines.

Grateful and special thanks to Jan Swarbrick who as copy editor has guided me through all the stages of writing and has researched plant names. In addition she has helped me in the garden and given me enormous support with her involvement in this book.

My thanks also to the many friends and visitors to the garden who have shown so much interest and enthusiasm over the years.

$\mathcal{I}$NDEX

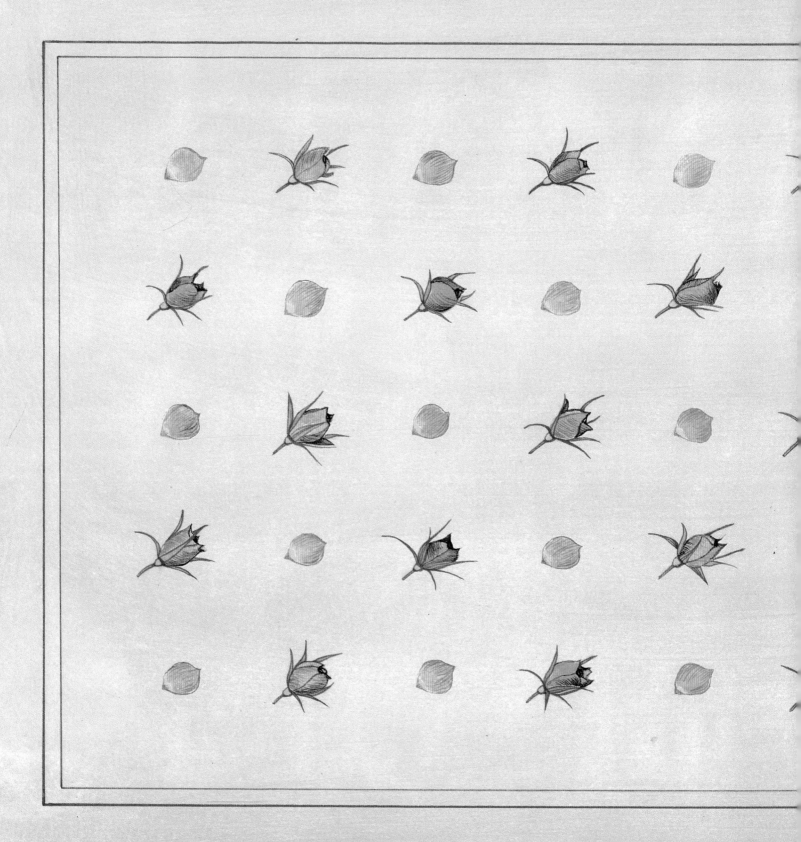